MATTERS
OF THE HEART

Matters of the Heart:
a 52-Week Scripture Memorization Challenge for Women

Carlie Kercheval

Learning to Speak Life Books™
store.LearningToSpeakLife.com

Copyright © 2016

ISBN-13: 978-0692706817

ISBN-10: 069270681X

Editing | Judy Hoch
ContentedAtHome.com/editor

Publishing and Design | MelindaMartin.me

Matters of the Heart

a 52-Week
Scripture Memorization
Challenge for Women

Carlie Kercheval

DEDICATION

This book is for every woman who longs to be free from the hurt and bondage of her past. I pray that you find peace in your heart through Jesus Christ. You are not alone, dear sister: I am right here in the trenches with you.

ENDORSEMENTS

The word of God is both practical and powerful, which is why I love Carlie's Scripture Memory Challenge. Carlie strategically connects targeted scripture memory with 52 heart and life challenges we commonly face as women. The result is a transparent, relatable resource that equips us for true transformation through the word of God.

Arabah Joy, ArabahJoy.com

Carlie has created a weekly plan that will help the woman who desires to go deeper with God. No matter how "busy" you are this 52-week memorization challenge will allow you the ability to hide more of God's Word in your heart.

Jamerrill Stewart,
The Encouraging Homeschool Mom
and FreeHomeschoolDeals.com

Being able to rattle off a few Scripture verses is nice, but if that's all your Scripture memorization consists of you're really missing out. *Matters of the Heart* contains solid Scripture, encouraging, relatable and applicable stories as well as 52 weekly challenges all designed to help you grow deeper in faith—not just knowledge. Would definitely recommend!

Brittany, EquippingGodlyWomen.com

Matters of the Heart is a great way to get a fresh focus on spiritual things. Each week Carlie shares a verse to memorize, along with an inspiring devotional and a practical application. Challenging and encouraging!

Judy Hoch, ContentedAtHome.com

As a busy mom of four, a devotional like *Matters of the Heart* is a wonderful addition to my alone time with God. I love how practical it is, and the wisdom that it imparts. Any mom will benefit from this book.

Rosanna Nguyen,
Co-Pastor Hope of Silicon Valley, hopesv.com

No matter what season of life you're in, or circumstance you might be facing, there is no greater calling on a woman's life than to love God and love others well. In Carlie Kercheval's book, *Matters of the Heart*, she shares God's Word, along with her own personal life experiences and faith story with absolute transparency and humility, inspiring and challenging women everywhere toward deeper faith. There is no better way to begin answering God's calling on our lives than to dig into our Bibles, soak in God's truths in the Scriptures and begin memorizing them. *Matters of the Heart* will take you on a year long Scripture memorizing journey you won't want to miss.

Megan Spires, DevotionalFamily.com

As a busy mom of six children I don't spend nearly enough time memorizing Scripture verses. This resource not only gives me short and easy to memorize verses, but also acts as a devotional book as well! I love how Carlie pulled it all together, to make it not only a practical resource, but a much needed devotional book to strengthen a woman's walk with God!

Caroline Allen, TheModestMomBlog.com

Memorizing Scripture is one of the best things we can do for our own personal spiritual growth and to become better wives and mothers. By walking through one Scripture memory verse a week (along with an uplifting meditation), Carlie will challenge you to meditate on and memorize God's Word for a whole year. Each verse is powerful, applicable, and short enough to learn quickly. I plan on memorizing them with my children!

Aliesha Caldwell, FeathersInOurNest.com

In the busyness of life, it's oftentimes things like memorizing Scripture that falls by the wayside. In *Matters of the Heart*, Carlie makes this important habit super simple. With weekly verses coupled with her own personal insight and thought-provoking questions to ponder, not only will memorizing Scripture become a habit you can finally conquer, the devotional-style writings will bless your heart.

Marcy Crabtree, BenAndMe.com

Matters of the Heart provides a terrific format to both memorize and implement the Scriptures. Carlie shares her personal experience in an easy conversational tone – even while digging into some tough topics! Although she doesn't pull any punches in discussing these struggles, each chapter is full of hope and victory through Christ. Carlie's words opened my heart to God's truth, allowing Him to show me where it needs to be applied in my own life. This devotional is for any woman who desires to walk closely with the Lord.

Kelli Becton, Frugal Mommas
and AdventureHomeschool.com

If you are looking for a great way to not only memorize Bible verses pertinent to your busy life as a mom, but to feast upon the words of Christ each and every week, you will love this challenge! Carlie does a great job of sharing personal insight and stories about each verse. She not only challenges you to memorize them, but to ponder specific, self-reflective questions as you do so. At the end of this challenge you will walk away not only more well-versed in scripture, but in spiritual power.

Katelyn Fagan, WhatsUpFagans.com

CONTENTS

INTRODUCTION

Why *Matters of the Heart?* God has been ministering to me for several years about the tenderness of a woman's heart. He has shown me the importance of balancing our tenderness of heart with strong biblical character. And as we know, Christ-like character can only be found in His Word and by His Spirit.

And so this 52-week memorization challenge was born.

This challenge was created with the modern-day Proverbs 31 woman in mind. In today's world we have to be extremely intentional about carving out time to connect with God. And I believe that rather than rushing our time in His Word, we should practice the habit of meditating on it so He can speak to the depths of our soul. That is why I have created a week-long challenge for each memory verse. It is my experience that the longer we meditate on God's Word, the more clearly we hear His voice.

I encourage you to take as long as you need to for each "weekly" challenge. While this challenge was created with a year-long timeframe in mind, please do not rush the process of memorization and connection with God. Use this challenge as a guideline and not an absolute. I believe that you will find your rhythm within the challenge, and that is what you should follow.

I have created two companion products to help you through your Scripture memory journey:

- Prayer + Reflection Journal - this is a great way to keep track of what God is showing you and keep track of answered prayers.

- 52 printable Scripture Cards - these cards will help aid memorization with visual memory.

You can purchase both of these in our online store: store.learningtospeaklife.com

Let's allow God to work on our hearts and expose things that are not pleasing to Him—and He will fill those desolate places with His love, mercy, and grace!

I cannot wait to hear how God changes your life as you begin to hide His Word in your heart!

xoxo,

Carlie Kercheval

Week 1:
Mothering From the Heart
{Pride}

The very first Scripture that we are going to commit to memory is Proverbs 21:2 (KJV):

Every way of a man [is] right in his own eyes: but the LORD pondereth the hearts.

I remember the first time I laid eyes on these words. I was a newly saved 22-year-old woman. And they hit me. *They hit me hard.*

So often I would think I was "right" and would fight hard for those "rights" I thought I had. Don't get me wrong. I'm not saying we shouldn't stand up for what's right, but I'm talking about the kind of right that is rooted in pride. I'm talking about *the need to always be right*. I'm referring to the type of right that isn't birthed out of a heart laid before Jesus.

That day, the conviction set in and healing began. God began to show me the importance of submitting that *need to always be right* to Him. He showed me how what I really longed for was the wisdom and justice that only He can give. He showed me the true intent of my heart—and it was ugly.

And then He began to heal me—to heal me through His Word, and give me hope for changing my heart. But it starts with knowing His Word. And so my quest to memorize Scripture began and has never ended.

I am so thankful that God helped me to see my weakness in this area, especially as it relates to being a mother. It can be tempting at times when raising our children to feel like we always have to be right. It can be tempting as a mother to fall victim to pride when we are tired and are having to discipline our child for the fiftieth time that day.

But despite how challenging it can be, if we submit our hearts to Him, we can walk victoriously in this area! Perfection? No. But a heart bent towards Jesus is the most beautiful heart in the world. And I know that we all desire to give our children God's best—and it all begins with the condition of our own heart!

Weekly Challenge

Commit this week's verse to memory.

As you ponder and meditate on this verse, ask yourself these questions:

1. Is the condition of my heart pleasing to the Lord?

2. What heart issues can I work on to make me a better mother (and a better person)?

Pray for the Lord to show you how you can continually submit *the need to be right* to Him and allow Him to fight your battles.

Write down any thoughts or prayers this week so you can keep track of how God is working in your life and the lives of others.

NOTES:

_____

_____

_____

_____

_____

_____

_____

_____

_____

_____

_____

_____

_____

_____

Week 2:
Mothering From the Heart
{Waiting}

This week's Scripture is Psalm 27:14 (KJV):

Wait on the LORD: be of good courage,
and he shall strengthen thine heart:
wait, I say, on the LORD.

Waiting. This is something that my human heart and mind are not accustomed to. Waiting is something that I've had to work very hard at submitting to the Lord. Waiting is something that I wholeheartedly wish we didn't have to do, but I have realized over time that God's timing is always precise. And it is through this precision that God has given me the ability to see His beauty in the process of purification, and for that, I am thankful.

I've realized as a mother that waiting is a gift—one that keeps on giving to the receiver of His promise. He plants seeds in us and brings them to pass when they are in due season. It's a beautiful process, really.

Be of good courage.

This is something at which I fail *often*. I allow my mind to get in the way in the midst of waiting and teeter with the temptation of being afraid. But He is merciful *and* patient with me. He strengthens me in the midst of the waiting, helping me to build character—all the while showing me how much He loves me. That's what a *good* parent does.

His example to me helps me become a better mother day by day. My Father God loves me through my faults and helps me become what His Word says I can be. In this case, it's becoming more patient. And in this process of learning patience, I am learning how to be of good courage. I am learning that when I allow Him to take control of my fears, I am, in turn, being courageous. This is also true in our relationship with our children.

As we continually develop patience in our lives, we can help our children to be more courageous in taking risks to see who they really are, and who God created them to be. This, my friends, is something I am willing to fight for. Will you fight with me?

WEEKLY CHALLENGE

Commit this week's verse to memory.

As you ponder and meditate on this verse, ask yourself these questions:

1. Am I waiting patiently for the promises of God?

2. How can I display more patience in situations where I am tempted to be impatient?

3. If you asked my children, would they say that I am patient?

Pray and ask the Lord to continuously show you how you can allow patience to have its perfect work in your heart and mind, specifically as it relates to motherhood.

Make it a point to look for an opportunity (or two, or three) where you can practice patience with your children (or other loved ones). Encourage those around you to practice patience as well.

Write down any thoughts or prayers this week so you can keep track of how God is working in your life and the lives of others.

NOTES:

_____

_____

_____

_____

_____

_____

_____

_____

_____

_____

_____

_____

_____

_____

_____

Week 3:
Mothering from the Heart
{Renewal}

This week's Scripture is Psalm 51:10 (KJV):

*Create in me a clean heart, O God; and
renew a right spirit within me.*

Every time I read, hear, or sing this verse, I am instantly broken. It doesn't matter what is or isn't going on in my life, Psalm 51:10 hits me hard. It doesn't matter if I am doing a morning devotional, worshiping in church, or just meditating on this verse; I am always shaken up after reading it. At first I didn't understand, but now I do.

I remember asking the Lord one day why Psalm 51:10 had such a profound impact on my life. I remember wondering if it was my "life verse" or if it had some upcoming grand showcase in the ministry He's called me to.

But it is neither.

God showed me that King David wrote these words out of an absolute state of brokenness—a place where only those who truly understand repentance and the condition of their human heart can relate to. Being broken (humbly submitted) before God is the only way we can truly see real heart-change.

But what does that have to do with me?

Everything.

God has called each one of us, dear mothers, to be broken before His glory. He is looking for moms who are able to recognize their shortcomings and submit them to Him so He can show them the right way to love their children. He is looking for moms who can come to Him and admit they need help and allow Him to renew them by His Holy Spirit. He is looking for those mothers who are not afraid to admit they don't have it all together on the inside nor the outside. He is looking for mothers who refuse to live a lie, but are actively seeking His truth. He is looking for those ready to receive His renewal. This, my dear friends, is what this verse has to do with me (and you).

Let's allow the Lord to create a clean heart in each one of us as He gently loves us and renews a right spirit (attitude, heart, and mind) within us. Let's allow Him to help us become the mother we've always wanted to be—not the one that we don't want to become. Let's allow Him to wipe away our tears, faults, guilt, and sinful ways so we can be free to parent our children as unto Him. He wants to renew you right now, momma; won't you let Him?

WEEKLY CHALLENGE

Commit this week's verse to memory.

As you ponder and meditate on Psalm 51:10 this week, ask yourself these questions:

1. What must I do right now to allow the Lord to cleanse my heart?

2. What can I give up that may be causing sin in my heart and mind?

3. Who can I ask to help me with this goal (accountability)?

Pray for the Lord to show you the difference between your idea of a "right" spirit and His holy definition.

Write down any thoughts or prayers this week so you can keep track of how God is working in your life and the lives of others.

NOTES:

_____

_____

_____

_____

_____

_____

_____

_____

_____

_____

_____

_____

_____

_____

_____

Week 4:
Mothering from the Heart
{ Purity }

This week's Scripture is Matthew 5:8 (KJV):

Blessed [are] the pure in heart: for they shall see God.

Purity. This is something that each one of us alone (without Christ) lacks. It isn't until we meet Jesus and begin to walk with Him that we start to understand the concept of biblical purity. And it is also through that relational understanding we are able to see just how impure we really are.

But there is hope.

Jesus said, "Blessed [are] the pure in heart: for they shall see God." But how can we be pure in heart when our sinful nature tries to take over our lives each day? How can we be pure in heart when we struggle with obeying God's commands? The truth is, we can't. However, sweet mommas, there is ONE who can and He dwells on the inside of each one of us who accepts Christ as our Savior. Who is this ONE I speak of? God's Holy Spirit.

I know that every mom out there who is reading this wants the very best for her child. It is just something that is built into our DNA—we want our children to be blessed. How much more does God want to bless His children? In Matthew 7:11 the Bible tells us: *If ye then, being evil, know how to give good gifts unto your children, how much more shall your Father which is in heaven give good things to them that ask him?* I believe this verse gives us a key to understand how we can begin our journey toward becoming pure in heart—simply ask God to help us.

When we ask the Lord to give us a pure heart, we are also asking Him to help us become better disciples, better mothers, better wives, and better friends. When we ask the Lord to help us become pure in our thoughts and in our hearts, we are giving our children a great example of the change that can come when we commit our hearts and ways to the Lord.

I don't know about you, but I am constantly striving for more and more purity in my heart, and I stand firm on His promise—I will see God! Hallelujah!

Weekly Challenge

Commit this week's verse to memory.

Be sure to pray and talk to the Lord to help you hear the voice of His Holy Spirit more clearly in your life. Also talk with God about ways that He can help you see how much you need His help in the area of biblical purity.

Consider fasting from something that is making your heart or mind impure in any area. Some ideas might be: fasting from sugary foods, fasting from television, fasting from impure conversations (gossip), or any of the endless areas in which we are tempted to sin each day.

Write down any thoughts or prayers this week so you can keep track of how God is working in your life and the lives of others.

NOTES:

_____

_____

_____

_____

_____

_____

_____

_____

_____

_____

_____

_____

_____

_____

_____

WEEK 5:
MOTHERING FROM THE HEART
{FORGIVENESS}

This week's Scripture is Leviticus 19:18 (KJV):

*Thou shalt not avenge, nor bear any
grudge against the children of thy people,
but thou shalt love thy neighbor as
thyself: I [am] the LORD.*

Forgiveness. It's something that every human who has walked the face of this earth will struggle with. If we're being honest, it's not easy to forgive someone who hurts your feelings. Nor is it easy to forgive someone who steals something valuable from your life, refusing to 'fess up to their wrongdoing. And if someone breaks our trust? Forget about it. *Or should we?*

I can think of a time or two where I was really hurt by someone and just plain didn't want to overlook nor forgive them. As a matter of fact, some of those offenses have come to me as a mother—and the offenders? My very own children!

Sound familiar?

While forgiving someone isn't the *easy* thing to do, it's the *right* thing to do. As a matter of fact, it is something that Christians *must* do if we are to be in right standing with God. Colossians 3:13 tells us: "Forbearing one another, and forgiving one another, if any man have a quarrel against any: even as Christ forgave you, so also *do* ye." Not only is it biblical to forgive, it also allows us to show our children and every one else the true nature of Christ! Isn't that a blessing?

Do you struggle with forgiving others? If so, I encourage you today to really focus on how God forgave you. Remember, in God's eyes no sin is greater than any other (with the exception of rejecting Christ), so we cannot really believe that we can be forgiven and someone else cannot. It simply isn't God's way.

I know that many of you out there are hurting and struggle with forgiveness right. I pray that you will allow God to take your hurt and replace it with His healing love as you walk out your journey of forgiveness. I pray that if the person you are struggling to forgive is yourself, that you will receive the grace that Christ gave when He died upon the cross so that you can be set free from the law of sin and death!

WEEKLY CHALLENGE

Commit this week's verse to memory.

If you harbor unforgiveness in your heart, pray and ask the Lord to show you how to begin the healing process that will lead you to true forgiveness. Even if you don't believe you have unforgiveness in your heart, pray and ask the Lord to reveal if there is anyone you need to forgive. God will show you.

Make intentional choices to show forgiveness to your children, spouse, or other family members this week. Sometimes it's difficult to show forgiveness to those we are closest to. Don't let the enemy destroy your relationships—rather, let God show you how to keep them strong!

Write down any thoughts or prayers this week so you can keep track of how God is working in your life and the lives of others.

NOTES:

_____

_____

_____

_____

_____

_____

_____

_____

_____

_____

_____

_____

_____

_____

_____

WEEK 6:
WALKING IN LOVE
{ACTION}

This week's Scripture is 1 John 3:18 (KJV):

*My little children, let us not love in word,
neither in tongue; but in deed and in
truth.*

If I am being honest, I can tell you that many times I have "loved" someone with my words but my actions told a different story. You know, telling someone you love them, only minutes later to hurt them by harsh words or undesirable actions. A bit hypocritical, isn't it? Unfortunately it happens more than I care to admit, but one thing is for sure—*it doesn't happen as much today as it did yesterday.*

And that's the key. Change doesn't happen overnight. It's the continual action of obedience that takes us where we need to go.

It's the action of obedience that touches the heart of our Father. It's the action of showing others we love them that reaches the very heart of God. It's the action of His grace that gives us the ability to love.

Will you embrace His love today?

Remember how it felt the first time you realized God loved you? The joy that it brought to your heart when you realized that He loved you so much that He sent His only son to die for you? Talk about loving with action!

It is in this place of love that we are empowered to give His love unconditionally to those God has called us to love.

Allow God's love to penetrate your heart and mind as you meditate on His Word. You will notice a difference in your relationships as you continue to put God first in all you do.

Let's go forth and spread God's love so that others might be saved!

WEEKLY CHALLENGE

Commit this week's verse to memory.

Challenge yourself to identify relationships in which you need to work on the action of walking in love. Once you pinpoint the relationship(s), write down some actions you can show each day to let them know you love them. Books that may help inspire you in this are *The Love Dare* and *The 5 Love Languages*.

Pray for God's grace as you take one step at a time to make the action of showing love a priority in your life. Ask Him to give you His heart for the people He has called you to influence. Ask Him to allow you to see His people just as He sees them.

Write down any thoughts or prayers this week so you can keep track of how God is working in your life and the lives of others.

NOTES:

_____

_____

_____

_____

_____

_____

_____

_____

_____

_____

_____

_____

_____

_____

_____

Week 7:
Walking in Love
{Reciprocation}

This week's Scripture is 1 John 4:19 (KJV):

We love him, because he first loved us.

He loves me. He loves me, even when I fall beneath His will. He loves me when I disobey. He loves me for me. He created me as a part of the body of Christ to uniquely fulfill a specific purpose. He loved me when I didn't even know who He was or acknowledge His name. God has always shown me love, and as a result I chose to receive and reciprocate His love. And you know what? The same is true for you. *He loves you.*

I am always taken aback when I read any of the gospel accounts of the crucifixion of our Lord. I am amazed at His unyielding love for humanity even though many people despised and rejected Him. I am always in awe of the fact that His unconditional love allowed Him to be unjustly accused and murdered so that we might be able to walk in a new covenant. I am inspired by the way He lived out His love through His actions in His short life here on earth. And so I do my best to reciprocate the love of God in everything that I do.

Have you received His love today, friend?

Will you allow His love to penetrate the darkest places in your heart? Will you accept and eventually learn how to love the way Christ loves? It is His will for us. If you fail (which we all will) to walk in love, don't give up; just keep trying. As with anything in life, you will grow stronger where you are weak so long as you allow Jesus to come in and show you what needs to be done.

Are you struggling to give and receive the love of God?

Perhaps it's healing from abusive relationships. Maybe you struggle to accept and give God's love because you were never shown any physical affection. What ever the reason, I encourage you today to meditate on 1 John 4:19, and allow God to perform His Word in your life. He will do it.

I am praying for you today, dear sister. And I love you, because He first loved me.

Weekly Challenge

Commit this week's verse to memory.

Search your heart and find an area in your life where you can improve on giving God's love to others. Make it a point this week (and hereafter) to find people that you can love on with the love of Christ. I guarantee you this will bless you just as much as it will bless the person you are loving on!

Pray and ask God to give you His love so that you can show His love to all you meet. And be sure to save some of that love for yourself.

Write down any thoughts or prayers this week so you can keep track of how God is working in your life and the lives of others.

NOTES:

_____

_____

_____

_____

_____

_____

_____

_____

_____

_____

_____

_____

_____

_____

_____

_____

Week 8:
Walking in Love
{Salvation}

This week's Scripture is John 3:16 (KJV):

*For God so loved the world, that he gave
his only begotten Son, that whosoever
believeth in him should not perish, but
have everlasting life.*

Imagine loving someone so much that you would give your only son so they might live. Imagine loving someone so much that you would do anything for them to enter into peace. Imagine a love so great that nothing can separate you from it—not even yourself. This, my friends, is the depth of God's love for us.

I remember when I first stumbled upon this verse at the beginning of my sophomore year of high school. I had a few friends that invited me to a Young Life group for high school students. I really didn't want to go, but had nothing else to do. At the time I was not a Christian and didn't realize that night God would plant a seed in my heart so deep that it would come to fruition several years later in the fall of 1998.

I will never forget the atmosphere of this dynamic and loving group. Everyone was smiling and seemed to be genuinely happy. It was a little odd to me. I remember sitting down in a group, and a kind-eyed woman told us to open up our Bibles to John 3:16. I didn't own a Bible so I looked on with my friend.

As the Young Life speaker read the verse I felt a chill go through my body like a bolt of lightening. I jerked. My friend looked at me and we both started to laugh. And although I was laughing, something had changed. And it wouldn't be until 6 years later that I realized what God had done. And it was then that I decided to believe in Him so that I might not perish, but have everlasting life. This, my friends, is His greatest gift to us, the gift of Salvation.

Have you received the LOVE of God and accepted the truth that Jesus, the Son of God, died for your sin? If you are uncertain, be sure to read the important truth about Salvation in Romans 10:9.

Imagine if we walked in love with the gift of God's Salvation in mind. I know for sure this world would be a much better place.

WEEKLY CHALLENGE

Commit this week's verse to memory.

I encourage you to sit and really think about what it would be like to sacrifice your only child or other loved one for others. How would that feel? That depth of sorrow God felt when He gave His only Son is something that is seemingly unfathomable. But on the opposite side of that deep sorrow is complete love and joy. This is worth meditating on and asking God to show you some truth to apply to your life from this verse.

Pray and ask the Lord to fill you with the kind of love that He created you to both give and receive. Ask Him to guide you into opportunities to share this same love that He displayed in John 3:16 (agape love) with those around you this week.

Write down any thoughts or prayers this week so you can keep track of how God is working in your life and the lives of others.

NOTES:

_____

_____

_____

_____

_____

_____

_____

_____

_____

_____

_____

_____

_____

_____

_____

Week 9:
Walking in Love
{Fear}

This week's Scripture is 1 John 4:18 (KJV):

There is no fear in love; but perfect love casteth out fear: because fear hath torment. He that feareth is not made perfect in love.

Have you ever been afraid? I mean *really* afraid? I know I have. I didn't grow up in the most desirable circumstances. From serious physical violence to mental and substance abuse, it seemed like fear was a permanent resident in my life. As time went on, I think I began to believe that fear was "normal" and began to just deal with it. It wasn't until I gave my life to Christ in 1998 that I realized how much pain I was truly in and began to experience the truth of 1 John 4:18.

I can tell you this: Perfect love (God) doesn't co-exist with torment. It wasn't until I surrendered everything I had (physically, mentally, and spiritually) to God that I realized how tormented and afraid I really was. I can also tell you that after I became a Christian my heart began to experience His peace, and I knew that I would never choose to go back to the state of mind I grew up in. *Ever.*

Can you relate with me, dear sister?

As I continue to progress in my relationship with God, I see more and more how His love has taken me from fear to faith. There have been countless occasions that I have been tempted to be afraid— from the death of a child to my husband fighting in war. But time and time again His love kept me walking in my faith rather than choosing to believe the lies that fear would tell me.

Perhaps you are struggling with fear right now. If you are, I am praying for you. I encourage you to allow God's perfect love to enter into your heart and mind to replace the fear that causes you harm with the joy that brings you peace. He is with you.

WEEKLY CHALLENGE

Commit this week's verse to memory.

If you are struggling with fear, I encourage you to speak 1 John 4:18 out loud (or silently meditate on it in your head) every time you are tempted to be fearful. The Bible tells us in Romans 10:17 that "faith cometh by hearing, and hearing by the word of God." When we actually speak the Word of life, we hear the Word of life, thus building up our faith.

Find someone you know who is struggling with fear this week and pray with them. Allow God to use you to speak life into their situation.

Write down any thoughts or prayers this week so you can keep track of how God is working in your life and the lives of others.

NOTES:

_____

_____

_____

_____

_____

_____

_____

_____

_____

_____

_____

_____

_____

_____

_____

WEEK 10:
REAL REPENTANCE
{CONFESSION}

This week's Scripture is 1 John 1:9 (KJV):

*If we confess our sins, he is faithful
and just to forgive us [our] sins, and to
cleanse us from all unrighteousness.*

The Bible teaches us that a very important part of real repentance (the true turning away from sin) is the confession of our transgressions—first to God Himself, then to anyone we may have sinned against. Real repentance isn't easy. No, as a matter of fact it can be painfully hard. But if we obey His Word, the temporary circumstances we are in begin to seem so trivial.

I've found that in the hardest times, when my pride is trying to keep me from turning away from my sin, that the blessing on the other side far outweighs the cost. I can honestly testify that God has never let me down when I confess my sin to Him. He has always replaced my anger, anxiety, or _____ (fill in the blank) with His peace when I confess my sin before Him. Not only has He forgiven us, He has given us the gift of peace when we are in right standing with Him.

Do you have a situation that you need to practice real repentance in? If so, I earnestly encourage you to confess your sin to God and allow Him to give you the strength and insight you need to walk away from that sin.

What may seem like an impossible situation to change can be transformed if you truly repent of your sin. Not only will God cause circumstances to shift when you confess your sin, He will also restore your heart. And this, my dear sisters, is worth its weight in gold!

Let the Lord take your unconfessed sin and replace it with the power of His forgiveness and peace!

WEEKLY CHALLENGE

Commit this week's verse to memory.

Dig deep into your heart this week. Ask the Lord to uncover any unconfessed sin in your life and make sure to confess it to God and anyone whom you may have hurt along the way. I promise you that your life will be blessed as a result.

Seek to bless someone this week that you may have had conflict with in the past. Maybe give them an unexpected word of encouragement or a hot meal. Let's make it a point to work out our salvation by moving beyond what's comfortable to our flesh!

Write down any thoughts or prayers this week so you can keep track of how God is working in your life and the lives of others.

NOTES:

_____

_____

_____

_____

_____

_____

_____

_____

_____

_____

_____

_____

_____

_____

_____

_____

_____

WEEK 11:
REAL REPENTANCE
{HEALING}

This week's Scripture is 2 Chronicles 7:14 (KJV):

If my people, which are called by my
name, shall humble themselves, and pray,
and seek my face, and turn from their
wicked ways; then will I hear from
heaven, and will forgive their sin,
and will heal their land.

One of the components of real repentance is the healing and restoration that comes afterward. When we truly turn from our sin (like we talked about last week) and confess our sin, it releases the hold that sin had on our lives, freeing that space up for God to consume. Anything that God touches is made whole. We see examples of God's healing power all throughout the New Testament. If we truly give God our heart, then He promises to make it new.

A new heart also will I give you, and a new spirit will I put within you, and I will take away the stony heart out of your flesh, and I will give you an heart of flesh. Ezekiel 36:26 (KJV)

Notice in this week's memory verse, the key to receiving our healing is found by doing these crucial things:

- humble ourselves

- pray

- seek Him

- turn from sin (repent)

It is only then, the verse tells us, that He will forgive our sin and heal our land.

I encourage you to make sure that you are positioning yourself to receive God's healing by taking the simple (or maybe not-so-simple) steps outlined in 2 Chronicles 7:14. I can testify with my whole being that if you do, He will make good on His promise and heal you tri-fold—mind, body, and spirit. These steps are crucial to your journey of repentance and should be a priority in your walk with God.

Think of some areas that you need to be healed and start thanking God for your healing today (receiving it by faith).

Remember that repentance is not a simple one-time thing; rather, it is a continuous lifestyle of submitting to Christ and allowing Him to build you and mold you into the amazing human being He has called you to be. Let Him heal you today, sweet one. No matter how hard it may seem to do the four steps above, I assure you that your obedience far outweighs any sacrifice you have to make along the way.

WEEKLY CHALLENGE

Commit this week's verse to memory.

Make a conscious effort this week to really seek the face of God. Don't ask Him for anything; just seek His presence and His heart. As you do this you will find Him and will experience His healing in a powerful way. Share with someone how God's healing power is at work in you!

Look for ways to humble yourself this week (and every day hereafter). Watch how God will use you in the most unexpected ways as you live out His Word.

Don't forget to share your healing journey with others as it may serve as a powerful encouragement and reminder of how much God loves them.

Write down any thoughts or prayers this week so you can keep track of how God is working in your life and the lives of others.

Notes:

_____

_____

_____

_____

_____

_____

_____

_____

_____

_____

_____

_____

_____

_____

_____

MATTERS OF THE HEART

WEEK 12: REAL REPENTANCE {CALLED}

This week's Scripture is Mark 2:17 (KJV):

When Jesus heard it, he saith unto them,
They that are whole have no need of the
physician, but they that are sick:
I came not to call the righteous, but
sinners to repentance.

Notice how Jesus makes the distinction in this verse that He came to call the sick (sinners) to repentance. This verse really changed my outlook on what it means to truly repent. It gave me the understanding that I needed to acknowledge that I was, in fact, sick with sin. I was infected with a virus the world could not cure—but salvation through Jesus Christ could. It was through this verse that Jesus showed me that through Him I could achieve real repentance and have the newness of life I had been searching for my entire life.

In the verses prior to this, the scribes and the Pharisees were questioning why Jesus was hanging out with tax collectors and sinners. Have you ever done that? Have you ever wondered why a person that didn't seem "fit" for service in the Kingdom of God was being blessed? I know in the past my wicked heart had thoughts like these. But God quickly corrected me and reminded me that I have no reason nor room to look at anyone and consider them unworthy of blessing. Only God can make that determination.

And as we know, we have all fallen short of the glory of God and need His Salvation to be free from the law of sin and death! Sinless? No, but able to discern what is and isn't acceptable in the moral standards of our Lord. And that, my friends, is where I want to be. Smack dab in the middle of His grace, not only receiving His grace, but allowing it to flow out of me freely into those God sees fit. After all, it's the sick who need a doctor, is it not?

Let's allow God to change our hearts this week as He calls us into closer communion with Him. Let's allow Him to use us to call others to His Kingdom who are still sick in their sin and haven't accepted His salvation. Let's determine to let the light of Christ shine through us as we are called to be His disciples and be fishers of men!

Weekly Challenge

Commit this week's verse to memory.

Make an effort to look for someone in your day-to-day life that seems to have been hurt or shunned by the church. Let God use you to minister to them and show them the love of Jesus right where they are at—no judgment—just love. *Just Jesus.* Watch how God uses you to bring that person's heart to Himself. It will not only bless them, it will also bless you as you realize how precious that person's life is to our Savior.

Pray for those who are sin-sick, asking God to draw them to Himself. Be willing to be His hands and feet this week as you pray.

Write down any thoughts or prayers this week so you can keep track of how God is working in your life and the lives of others.

Notes:

_____

_____

_____

_____

_____

_____

_____

_____

_____

_____

_____

_____

_____

_____

Week 13:
Real Repentance
{Comfort}

This week's Scripture is Acts 2:38 (KJV):

Then Peter said unto them, Repent, and be baptized every one of you in the name of Jesus Christ for the remission of sins, and ye shall receive the gift of the Holy Ghost.

I remember the day I gave my life to Christ. It was something fierce. It was a day that I realized just how sin-sick my heart really was and how full of pain and condemnation my life had been up until that very moment. I was full of guilt-ridden hatred for myself and the world around me and was in dire need of intervention.

But then it happened.

I asked Christ into my heart and received the gift of the Holy Spirit. The promise in Acts 2:38 echoes what Jesus promised his disciples in John 14:15-17:

¹⁵If ye love me, keep my command-ments. ¹⁶And I will pray the Father, and he shall give you another Comforter, that he may abide with you for ever; ¹⁷*Even* the Spirit of truth; whom the world cannot receive, because it seeth him not, neither knoweth him: but ye know him; for he dwelleth with you, and shall be in you.

And it's true. He did send us a Comforter—the Holy Spirit. And the world cannot receive the Holy Spirit because it's a gift available only to those who accept Jesus Christ as their Savior. It's a part of the won-derful gift of Salvation found only through Christ. And the beautiful thing? The Comforter not only fills us with God's love, peace, and joy, but He is always there to help us keep our convictions strong and give us wisdom for the narrow path God has carved just for you and me.

Have you asked the Jesus into your heart and ac-cepted His salvation? Have you been baptized? If not, I encourage you to follow your heart and accept Jesus as your Savior. It really is quite a simple thing to do. And baptism following our Salvation is just an outward expression of our new-found love for Jesus. There is something so powerful about telling everyone that you love Jesus through the symbolic act of water baptism!

WEEKLY CHALLENGE

Commit this week's verse to memory.

If you have been putting off the act of faith to receive Jesus as Lord and Savior, don't wait any longer. Ask Him into your heart today. And if you haven't been water baptized, I encourage you to pray and ask the Lord to show you the importance of this symbolic act of faith modeled for us in Matthew 3:13-17.

Do you know someone who could use comfort in their heart and life right now? If so, pray for them and make it a point to show them a practical act of God's love this week. And if you are unsure, just pray for those who need God's comfort. Someone, somewhere, always needs comfort. Let's love on God's people (and that means both Christians and non-Christians alike as He loves us ALL).

Write down any thoughts or prayers this week so you can keep track of how God is working in your life and the lives of others.

NOTES:

_____

_____

_____

_____

_____

_____

_____

_____

_____

_____

_____

_____

_____

_____

_____

_____

WEEK 14:
THE JOY OF THE LORD
{STRENGTH}

This week's Scripture is Nehemiah 8:10 (KJV):

*Then he said unto them, Go your way, eat
the fat, and drink the sweet, and send
portions unto them for whom nothing
is prepared: for this day is holy unto our
Lord: neither be ye sorry; for the joy of
the Lord is your strength.*

In Nehemiah 8, God called on His people during the Feast of Tabernacles to be joyful. Ezra the priest had led the people in the reading of the law and worship. It was during this time that Ezra said the famous words of Nehemiah 8:10. And the people received the joy of the Lord because their hearts were tender before the Lord. This is an important part of receiving anything from God: We must humble ourselves before Him by getting into His Word, praying, and worshipping. This opens up the doors of our heart and allows God to work in us.

This Scripture has always given me great joy simply because it reminds me that we are to be the hands and feet of Jesus, serving His people out of the abundance of His blessing in our lives. It also reminds me that we do not need to be bitter or angry about our circumstances, but rather allow God's strength to bring us joy as we take Him at His Word.

One of the most amazing things about Jesus is the simple fact that He is faithful to perform His Word. What an honor it is to serve a God who doesn't lie and gives His people true hope and vision for their uniquely appointed lives.

Remember, dear sister, that true joy can only be found in Jesus. A large part of this stems from the fact that through Him we can gain the perspective we need to see life in light of eternity rather than from the carnal, circumstantial perspective. This eternal insight gives us real hope and purpose with which God can lead others right back to Himself! True joy is a blessing and I'm so thankful for this gift from the Lord!

Weekly Challenge

Commit this week's verse to memory.

Identify an area or two in your life where you have not allowed the joy of the Lord to be your strength. Pray and ask God to help you receive His joy in place of your pain, worry, or other unhealthy emotion. He will do it!

Allow the Lord to use you as His joy toward someone else this week. Watch the way God will use you to bless His people with His infectious joy as you submit yourself to Him in this area!

Write down any thoughts or prayers this week so you can keep track of how God is working in your life and the lives of others.

NOTES:

_____

_____

_____

_____

_____

_____

_____

_____

_____

_____

_____

_____

_____

_____

Week 15:
The Joy of the Lord
{Fullness}

This week's Scripture is Psalm 16:11 (KJV):

Thou wilt shew me the path of life: in thy presence is fulness of joy; at thy right hand there are pleasures for evermore.

Fullness as defined on dictionary.com is: *the quality or state of being full.* And that's exactly what we'll find in the presence of the Lord: joy to the point of being full. Have you experienced joy before? Perhaps you experienced joy the moment you accepted Jesus as your Savior or found out that you were having a baby. Maybe you experienced joy when your mom or dad told you they loved you. Whatever it is that has brought you joy in this life, imagine having that feeling all of the time. *Sit and really imagine that for a minute.*

That is exactly what you'll experience in God's presence: complete joy—no sorrow or sadness. Isn't that a beautiful promise? There are so many ways that we can be in His presence:

- worship

- prayer

- reading His Word

- obedience when we hear His voice

- fellowship with other believers

God is so amazing that He has given us joy as a manifestation of the fruit of the Spirit. It is ours for the taking if we'll position ourselves to receive it.

Will you do that today, dear sister? Will you let Him fill you with His joy?

If the answer is yes, get ready for an amazing experience that will take you deeper in your relationship with God and people.

WEEKLY CHALLENGE

Commit this week's verse to memory.

Write down things in your life that cause you stress, pain, or anger. Pray and ask the Lord to give you joy in place of the things that cause you to not be joyful. Ask Him for the wisdom to enter into His presence so you can receive the fullness of His joy in your life. Watch and see that He will do it if you are careful to obey His instruction.

Make it a point this week to really get into the presence of the Lord. If you are having trouble doing so, ask your pastor or another trusted Christian friend to pray with you about this. God will show you exactly what you need to do in order to dwell in His presence. It will change your life!

Write down any thoughts or prayers this week so you can keep track of how God is working in your life and the lives of others.

NOTES:

_____

_____

_____

_____

_____

_____

_____

_____

_____

_____

_____

_____

_____

_____

WEEK 16:
THE JOY OF THE LORD
{ASK}

This week's Scripture is John 16:24 (KJV):

Hitherto have ye asked nothing in my name: ask, and ye shall receive, that your joy may be full.

In John 16, Jesus was preparing His disciples for His departure. One of the many things he talked to His disciples about was the simple fact that He was going to be departing and returning to the Father, and that the Holy Spirit would finish the work He had begun. In talking to the disciples about His Holy Spirit, He also let them know that the sorrow they would experience when He was gone would turn into joy. A key component of receiving that joy is by asking (in prayer) for joy (or any other good gift) in Jesus' name.

Have you ever faced a tough situation that left you feeling helpless, sad, angry, or even hopeless? I have. And in those times I have disciplined myself to pray and ask God to give me His joy in place of the negative feelings my heart sometimes harbors. The great news is that when Jesus left his physical body and returned to heaven, He left us with a gift. That gift is the Holy Spirit who gives us peace, joy, wisdom, and all that is good while we are still here in the flesh. I can think of countless instances where God's Holy Spirit gave me joy where there was sorrow. Can you?

I'd like to encourage you today to really allow the Holy Spirit to replace your sorrow with joy. After all, joy is a fruit of the Spirit (see Galatians 5), and I don't know about you, but I'd like to display the fruit of the Spirit as often as I can in my life!

Let's decide together that we are going to discipline ourselves to walk in God's joy rather than any other fleeting emotion that can cause us to take our eyes off of Jesus. Let's determine together, sweet sister, that God's joy will radiate out of us and into the lives of others! Let's show Jesus to all we meet! Hallelujah!

Weekly Challenge

Commit this week's verse to memory.

Identify areas of your life where you are experiencing sorrow. Pray and ask God to give you His joy in the name of Jesus. Watch and see how He will do it! Remember, though, that you have to allow God to do His work in your heart and life, so make sure you are willing.

Make it a point to let the joy of the Lord at work in your life touch someone else this week. It will bless you to see just how much God loves His people when you see the fruit of joy literally changing the atmosphere and hearts of the people around you!

Write down any thoughts or prayers this week so you can keep track of how God is working in your life and the lives of others.

NOTES:

_____

_____

_____

_____

_____

_____

_____

_____

_____

_____

_____

_____

_____

_____

_____

WEEK 17:
THE JOY OF THE LORD
{TEMPTATION}

This week's Scripture is James 1:2-4 (KJV):

*My brethren, count it all joy when ye fall
into divers temptations; Knowing this,
that the trying of your faith worketh
patience. But let patience have her perfect
work, that ye may be perfect and entire,
wanting nothing.*

Temptation is a struggle for every human on the face of this earth. While I don't like to admit it, I have many struggles of my own that I am tempted to give in to every day. I'm tempted to feel like a terrible wife. I'm tempted to feel like a horrible mother. I'm tempted to yell at my children when I am angry. I'm tempted to think that I am insignificant and can't possibly have anything good to bring into the world. I'm tempted to believe that I am not giving my all to the assignments God has given me. And the list of temptations goes on and on....

Can you relate?

One thing that the Lord has taught me is that when I am tempted to sin, it is because I am walking in self-reliance rather than reliance on Him. I've learned to appreciate the testing and trying of my faith as I acknowledge that if I continue to get up every day and give my life back over to Him, then everything I go through is purifying me. And in addition to this, I really have learned to rejoice in my temptation and suffering because it all ends up glorifying Him in the end.

And even though I do not serve God to gain anything more than His peace and love, I have realized that a by-product of serving Him through the good and bad times has been being more whole than I could have ever imagined. I can honestly say that I see how patience is having her perfect work in my heart and mind (don't get me wrong, I still struggle, but there is fruit). The evidence of this is sprinkled all over my life.

I encourage you, dear sister, to learn to rejoice in your temptations and suffering as it produces strong biblical character in you. Allow the Lord to be praised no matter what circumstance you face today. I'm praying for you and am walking right beside you.

WEEKLY CHALLENGE

Commit this week's verse to memory.

Seek to resolve any areas in your life where you are not turning temptation over to the Lord. Then, once you've identified these areas, rejoice because you know He has given you the victory through Christ Jesus!

Pray for a family member, friend, church member, or stranger who is currently bogged down by bad choices. Pray that God's joy would saturate his or her heart, mind, and circumstance, and that He would make Himself known amidst the person's trial.

Write down any thoughts or prayers this week so you can keep track of how God is working in your life and the lives of others.

Notes:

_____

_____

_____

_____

_____

_____

_____

_____

_____

_____

_____

_____

_____

_____

Week 18:
The Joy of the Lord
{Morning}

This week's Scripture is Psalm 30:5 (KJV):

For his anger endureth but a moment; in his favour is life: weeping may endure for a night, but joy cometh in the morning.

Every time I read Psalm 30:5, my heart leaps for joy. I mean, literally jumps for joy. I can feel so many pleasant emotions including love, hope, and peace giving me the fuel I need to move forward in my current circumstances. I cannot begin to tell you how many times I have referenced this verse during some of the deepest, darkest seasons of my life. This verse has literally given me hope that my morning will come. And it always does.

Are you in need of hope?

I know I am.

One of the takeaways from Psalm 30:5 that has continuously sustained me is the promise of joy coming when the season of testing has come to an end. Because eventually every season does come to an end—both good and bad. I am encouraged that the Lord not only gives us His joy in the process, but He also grants us His unmerited favor.

You see, dear sister, even when you can't "see" it, God's favor is all around you and upon your life simply because His Word is true. Be that as it may, you must decide in your heart to take Him at His Word and do whatever it takes to keep your faith in Jesus strong.

No matter what you are facing today, His joy will come in the morning. Make the decision to trust and believe that your morning is just on the horizon.

Hallelujah!

Weekly Challenge

Commit this week's verse to memory.

Take the time to reflect back on your life during times of hardship and how the Lord brought you through. Thank Him for His goodness and ask Him for His favor and wisdom to guide you in all you do, today and every day.

Confess Psalm 30:5 out loud as often as possible to build up your faith. The Bible tells us to meditate on His Word both day and night. Watch and see the benefits of storing up the Word in your heart!

Write down any thoughts or prayers this week so you can keep track of how God is working in your life and the lives of others.

NOTES:

_____

_____

_____

_____

_____

_____

_____

_____

_____

_____

_____

_____

_____

_____

WEEK 19:
GOD IS FAITHFUL
{CALLED}

This week's Scripture is 1 Thessalonians 5:24 (KJV):

Faithful is he that calleth you, who also will do it.

I love the fact that I can *always* count on God. I love the fact that no matter what I do or don't do, He is faithful. And you know what else I love, dear sister? I love the fact that God has called each one of us to cleave unto Him and will always do what His Word promises.

God *is* faithful.

Even when the storms of life are beating us so badly that we can barely stand, *God is faithful*. Even when bad things happen to us and to those around us, *God is faithful*. Even when we fail miserably and feel like God shouldn't, wouldn't, or couldn't love us—*He is faithful.* And I have learned to rest in His faithfulness. It is in God's faithfulness that I find everything I need. I know for certain that His truth will guide me into the wisdom I need for daily life and service to Him.

As we abide in His faithfulness and do our very best to follow His commands, we can rest assured that we will always see His hand at work in our lives. And this, dear sister, is something for which to be thankful!

Will you rest in His faithfulness today?

God is calling you into a deeper understanding of who He is in your life. I encourage you do listen to the call and follow it with your whole heart. No need to worry about anything because His faithfulness with carry you through!

WEEKLY CHALLENGE

Commit this week's verse to memory.

What has God called you to do? Not the "title" of your calling, but even the day-to-day things. Ask God what He's calling you to do today and be obedient. Watch and see how His faithfulness flows into your day as you walk in the things He has called you to do.

Target an area of your life in which you tend to rely on your own strength, and not God's faithfulness. Submit this area to the Lord and thank Him for His faithfulness in your life!

Write down any thoughts or prayers this week so you can keep track of how God is working in your life and the lives of others.

Notes:

_____

_____

_____

_____

_____

_____

_____

_____

_____

_____

_____

_____

_____

_____

_____

WEEK 20:
GOD IS FAITHFUL
{HOLD FAST}

This week's Scripture is Hebrews 10:23 (KJV):

Let us hold fast the
profession of our faith without wavering;
(for he is faithful that promised;)

I cannot count the number of times that I have been in a holding pattern waiting for God to fulfill His promise. Now don't misread what I wrote. I am certainly not implying that God is slow or unfaithful; rather I am saying that I've been challenged in my faith as I wait for His promises to unfold.

And that's just it. God's promises are true, but in the waiting is where He does some of His most beautiful work, His life-changing refinement process. While it isn't always fun to be waiting, one thing is certain: *God is faithful.*

Have you been there before? Waiting on God and your faith begins to shake like muscles that have been worked until the point of failure? I know I have. And there is beauty in the waiting if we will just *hold fast*.

Holding fast isn't easy when there are bills to pay *and* mouths to feed *and* terminal diagnoses given *and* eviction notices served. Holding fast isn't easy when you find out that the job your spouse has held for twenty years is coming to an end for no reason. And I know we can all think of about one hundred other scenarios where holding fast isn't easy.

But dear sister, holding fast is a part of the muscle of faith that we must develop to have a thriving walk with our Jesus.

So as you go about your daily life, remember to always hold fast to the profession of your faith, because God is faithful!

WEEKLY CHALLENGE

Commit this week's verse to memory.

Write down some things that you are believing God for. Look up some Scriptures to confess over your seed (of faith) while you are holding fast to God's promises. Watch your faith grow and your promise unfold as you sow into building your faith for His glory!

Speak this week's Scripture out loud several times a day, replacing the word "us" with "me." Make it a personal confession and watch how your circumstances will change and your faith will increase!

Write down any thoughts or prayers this week so you can keep track of how God is working in your life and the lives of others.

Notes:

_____

_____

_____

_____

_____

_____

_____

_____

_____

_____

_____

_____

_____

_____

Week 21:
God Is Faithful
{Abideth}

This week's Scripture is 2 Timothy 2:13 (KJV):

If we believe not, yet he abideth faithful:
He cannot deny himself.

One of the greatest gifts that I have discovered in my Christian journey is summed up so well in this week's memory verse: *He cannot deny himself.* I believe it is this simple truth that many Christians miss, and as a result they find themselves unhappy and, in some cases, walking away from their faith.

The truth in 2 Timothy 2:13 helped produce a pivotal point in my walk with Jesus. I actually know that regardless of my inability to be faithful, God is still faithful. Even when He has asked something of me and I disobey, God is still faithful. And what's even more beautiful about this is the simple fact that it is for only one reason that God is faithful: *He cannot deny himself.*

As we learn throughout the New Testament, God is love. And it is the very essence of love that doesn't allow God to do anything bad. As James 1:17 (KJV) tells it:

> *Every good gift and every perfect gift is from above, and cometh down from the Father of lights, with whom is no variableness, neither shadow of turning.*

Did you see that? God is good and perfect and there is never any variant of His nature. *Ever.*

If you gain anything out of this week's memory verse and devotional, sweet sister, I pray that it is a deeper revelation of just exactly *who* God is. There is not one of us that can't stand to know more of Him and His ways. Let it be a lifelong quest to pursue all that is good, allowing His faithfulness to guide us into all truth—which is His love.

Rest in knowing that God is faithful regardless of whether you make a mistake or not. He is just good. And He loves you unconditionally.

WEEKLY CHALLENGE

Commit this week's verse to memory.

Take the time out this week (and continue to do so hereafter) to really notice how faithful God is in your life and the lives of those around you. Let Him show you exactly who He is in the here and now. Open up your heart so wide that all you can see is His faithfulness, and not your own mess. It will change you, I promise.

Write down three areas (or more) in which you need to see God's faithfulness. Pray and ask Him to reveal Himself strong in those particular areas. Make it a lifelong habit to thank Him every day for being faithful in your life.

Write down any thoughts or prayers this week so you can keep track of how God is working in your life and the lives of others.

NOTES:

_____

_____

_____

_____

_____

_____

_____

_____

_____

_____

_____

_____

_____

_____

Week 22:
God Is Faithful
{Great}

This week's Scripture is Lamentations 3:22-23 (KJV):

22 It is of the Lord's mercies that we are not consumed, because his compassions fail not. 23 They are new every morning: great is thy faithfulness.

G reat is Thy Faithfulness has always been one of my favorite hymns. Every time I sing this song, no matter the season of life I am in, I weep. Simply knowing the only reason that I am not consumed by my sin is because He is faithful is enough to break me—every.single.time.

Can you think of a time where God's compassion showed itself strong in your life? I can think of many, many times this has been true. I will never forget God's compassion and mercy during the loss of our second child nearly eleven years ago. It was when I gave birth to a stillborn son, baby Noah, that God's compassion and mercy consumed my soul so I could get through the next year all alone.

It was exactly 7 days after the loss of our baby boy, Noah, that my husband was shipped off to war in Iraq for a year. Without God's faithfulness showing up in my life that day—and every single minute of every hour of that entire twelve months apart—I would have been consumed by my sin. But because His mercies are new every morning, I had the hope that my promise for a son would still come to pass—and it did—two-fold.

It is important that we never forget the role that God's faithfulness plays in our day-to-day lives. Without the perspective of understanding how faithful God is, we cannot fully live out all He has intended for us upon this earth. And I don't know about you, but I don't want to exist apart from God's faithfulness.

It is in His faithfulness that I've found the ability to love, live, and enjoy the gift of life. It is through His faithfulness that I've been able to walk out my life with hope, peace, and joy. And it is His faithfulness that keeps me going when I feel like I am going to fall apart. His faithfulness is the very reason that I am free—and for that, I am grateful!

WEEKLY CHALLENGE

Commit this week's verse to memory.

Sit down and talk with your spouse, friend, or loved one about what God's faithfulness means to you. Sometimes it helps to verbalize and share our testimony—as well as to hear another person's testimony—about God's faithfulness to build up our faith in Him.

Pray that God would allow you to be used as evidence of His faithfulness in the lives of others. Look for opportunities to share His faithfulness with those who need it. I guarantee it will bless you more than you think!

Write down any thoughts or prayers this week so you can keep track of how God is working in your life and the lives of others.

Notes:

_____

_____

_____

_____

_____

_____

_____

_____

_____

_____

_____

_____

_____

_____

_____

Week 23:
His Strength
{Weakness}

This week's Scripture is 2 Corinthians 12:9 (KJV):

*And he said unto me, My grace is sufficient
for thee: for my strength is made perfect
in weakness. Most gladly therefore will
I rather glory in my infirmities, that the
power of Christ may rest upon me.*

I cannot express to you how much joy fills my spirit every time I read 2 Corinthians 12:9. To know that God's grace is sufficient is more than comforting, but to know that His strength is made perfect in weakness? I couldn't be more thrilled. Because you see, if we are being honest with ourselves, we are weak more often than we are strong. Sure, it sounds great to say, "Why yes, I am a strong person." But the reality is that no one is strong in and of themselves.

We might be good at pretending we are fine or faking that we have it all together, but that is not strength—that is weakness. If we were strong, we wouldn't need a Savior to pull us out of our sin-gripped lives. If we were strong, we wouldn't be on our knees praying to God for justice, peace, forgiveness, favor, well...you get the picture.

But there *is* a real strength that sustains us in our darkest hour. There is a real strength that shows us our imperfections and teaches us how to love ourselves anyhow. There is a real strength that is made perfect in our weakness, and it is the strength that God gives. If you will just admit you are weak and hand it over to Jesus, He will give you the ability to rise above your circumstances.

Will you accept His strength today? Will you give Him the chance to show you that He is God and how amazing it is to walk in His strength? Will you let God recharge you and allow you to walk toward the fullness of blessing in your life? I surely hope so, dear sister.

Whatever you are facing right now that may be pulling on you and stealing your joy—allow God to step in and take over. Allow His loving-kindness to bring you the wisdom, comfort, and peace you desire. Let the Omnipotent God battle on your behalf. Let His strength be made perfect in your weakness. It is when we hand over our weaknesses to God, and only then, that His strength can be made perfect in our lives. Let Him do it today.

Weekly Challenge

Commit this week's verse to memory.

Name three areas that you are weak in. Be honest with yourself. Take those three areas to the Lord in prayer and ask Him to show Himself strong in your weakness.

Make it a point to find a Scripture(s) that you can confess over your biggest area of weakness to build your faith and character. Watch God come in and watch His Word completely change your situation!

Write down any thoughts or prayers this week so you can keep track of how God is working in your life and the lives of others.

NOTES:

_____

_____

_____

_____

_____

_____

_____

_____

_____

_____

_____

_____

_____

_____

WEEK 24:
HIS STRENGTH
{CHRIST}

This week's Scripture is Philippians 4:13 (KJV):

I can do all things through Christ which strengtheneth me.

Very few days have gone by in my walk as a Christian where I didn't have to quote or pray this Scripture. Countless times every day I find myself in a position that I simply cannot overcome in my own strength. When I feel like giving up, Philippians 4:13 always gives me the comfort and strength I need to face whatever challenges the day may hold.

Have you ever felt like giving up? Have you ever wanted to just walk away from something because it seemed too hard? I have. But I learned a long time ago that hiding God's Word in my heart would help me overcome the temptation to give up, and give me the strength and wisdom I needed to walk through every season of life with complete and total victory.

What are you facing today, dear sister, that is tempting you to give up?

I encourage you to look that thing right in the face and boldly declare: I can do ALL things through Christ Jesus! Repeat this until you believe it and your spirit is filled with the strength that only God can give!

There is nothing more powerful than the Word of God, and when we discipline ourselves to hide His Word in our heart, we will always have the victory! Hallelujah!

Weekly Challenge

Commit this week's verse to memory.

Identify the areas in your life where you feel like giving up. Confess Philippians 4:13 over and over until you see your faith rise to the occasion, and wait with great expectancy for God's wisdom in your situation.

Commit to praying this verse over your family, church family, co-workers, and anyone else for whom you feel led to pray. Watch God's Word take root and change the lives of those around you!

Write down any thoughts or prayers this week so you can keep track of how God is working in your life and the lives of others.

NOTES:

_____

_____

_____

_____

_____

_____

_____

_____

_____

_____

_____

_____

_____

Week 25:
His Strength
{Renew}

This week's Scripture is Isaiah 40:31 (KJV):

But they that wait upon the Lord shall renew their strength; they shall mount up with wings as eagles; they shall run, and not be weary; and they shall walk, and not faint.

Have you ever been in a season of life where you needed the Lord to renew your strength? Perhaps you are in one right as you read these very words. Maybe you just finished a season of weariness or are about to enter into one. I'm here to encourage you to *hold on.*

I must confess that I've been in many situations where I was weary and wondered where I had gone wrong. And for the longest time, I would sit and wonder why all my hard work seemed to amount to nothing but stress and dead ends. As I cried out to the Lord,

He would take me back to Isaiah 40:31 every time, showing me that I was not waiting upon Him but attempting to do things in my own strength. The Bible is very clear that we must not lean on our own understanding, but rather glean from the wisdom of God, and He will direct us in the path of righteousness.

The promises found in this verse are such an encouragement to me. To know that if I wait on the Lord for His guidance and wisdom that He will renew my strength gives me a hope that is indescribable. Every time I think about mounting up with wings as an eagle I am overtaken by the absolute freedom that brings. I imagine myself soaring freely above everything—soaring above every circumstance, soaring above every sin that hinders, rising above all the negativity in the world, soaring with my Jesus.

I love how the verse promises me that I will run this race He has called me to and not grow weary so long as I wait upon Him.

Will you wait upon Him today, sister?

Let's wait together!

WEEKLY CHALLENGE

Commit this week's verse to memory.

Are you committed to waiting on the Lord? Or are you prone to go ahead of His plans? This week, take a deep, hard look into your life and submit any areas in which you are going ahead of His plan, asking Him to show you His will.

Connect with some of your friends and family who are waiting on God for something. Agree in prayer that He will do what He said He would do and watch His perfect will take shape in your lives!

Write down any thoughts or prayers this week so you can keep track of how God is working in your life and the lives of others.

NOTES:

_____

_____

_____

_____

_____

_____

_____

_____

_____

_____

_____

_____

_____

_____

_____

Week 26:
His Strength
{Soul}

This week's Scripture is Psalm 138:3 (KJV):

In the day when I cried thou answeredst me, and strengthenedst me with strength in my soul.

Sometimes it's easy to forget to listen for God's answer when we call out to Him. I know there have been many times (and I'm sure many more before my life is over) where I've missed walking in God's strength simply because I didn't listen. However, when I listen He has always answered me—wrapping His arms around me and clothing me in His strength.

Time after time as I've cried out to the Lord, He has answered me and been faithful to give me the strength I need to face any situation. It is always amazing to me how quickly the Lord answers when we are listening for His voice. There used to be a time when I felt like God wasn't there—like He abandoned me. But through many trials and life experiences I've learned that God is always there, but we don't often hear because we are too busy being noisy. You know, the noise we fill our minds with that has nothing to do with God's Word:

He said, she said.

I'm not good enough.

Why do they always get what they want?

I wish I could be like her.

I'm not worth anything.

If God would just give me (insert anything) I'd be happy.

and so on and so on...

But what if I told you that God will answer you when you cry out—so long as you are listening for His voice? What if I told you that I've experienced this truth in my life again and again since I accepted His call on my life in the fall of 1998? Would you believe me?

I encourage you to call out to God each and every time you feel weak, insignificant, insecure, or scared.

And when you do, if you listen for His still small voice, you will hear it, and He will give you the wisdom you need to strengthen your soul. Don't give up, dear sister, His strength will bring you through.

WEEKLY CHALLENGE

Commit this week's verse to memory.

Confess Psalm 138:3 out loud until you believe it in your heart that God will answer you when you call.

Be sure to create some "quiet" time for yourself each day. Even if that means a five-minute prayer or reading your devotional when you are able throughout the day, that's all right. It's not the amount of time that matters but simply the fact that you make the time. God knows your heart and He will bless you right where you are at.

Write down any thoughts or prayers this week so you can keep track of how God is working in your life and the lives of others.

NOTES:

_____

_____

_____

_____

_____

_____

_____

_____

_____

_____

_____

_____

_____

_____

WEEK 27:
GOD, OUR PROVIDER
{ALL}

This week's Scripture is Philippians 4:19 (KJV):

*But my God shall supply all your need
according to his riches in glory by
Christ Jesus.*

*E*very time I read, speak, or hear this verse my heart leaps for joy. Just the thought of knowing that God will supply all my need is one that has continued to give me great peace over the last 18+ years on my journey with Christ.

I looked up the word "need" in this verse in my *Strong's Exhaustive Concordance* and in this particular verse *need* refers to: *employment, business, lack, necessary, necessity, need, use, want.* What I see there is the simple fact that God wants to bless us in absolutely every area of our lives—not just spiritually. *Isn't that comforting?*

To know we have a God that actually cares about blessing us with the needs that our physical existence demands is a great source of encouragement for me.

Whenever I am tempted to worry or think about what we need, I meditate on this verse. Anytime I see a great need for those around me, I pray this verse. Every time I am faced with an uncertainty in our lives, I pray and confess this verse. Philippians 4:19 has held me up countless times and I pray that it does the very same for you and your precious family.

God's Word is living and active and He loves you far more than you can imagine. As badly as you want to provide for your family, He wants to (and has already) provide for you. It's just a matter of allowing Him to show you the steps to get there. And once He does and you obey, you will find His provision waiting for you.

Will you rest in His provision today?

Whatever the need you have today, God can and will fill it.

WEEKLY CHALLENGE

Commit this week's verse to memory.

Write down some areas that you are in need of God's provision. Pray and ask Him to show Himself strong in these areas. Watch as He gives you what you need out of His riches and glory!

How has God shown you that He will supply all your need? Share your testimony with someone today and watch how God builds their confidence in Him.

Confess this verse out loud over and over to build up your own faith and to help with memory.

Write down any thoughts or prayers this week so you can keep track of how God is working in your life and the lives of others.

NOTES:

_____

_____

_____

_____

_____

_____

_____

_____

_____

_____

_____

_____

_____

Week 28:
God, Our Provider
{Ask}

This week's Scripture is Matthew 7:11 (KJV):

If ye then, being evil, know how to give good gifts unto your children, how much more shall your Father which is in heaven give good things to them that ask him?

For those of us who have children, this Scripture really hits home. The innate desire to bless our children is undeniable. From the moment that my first child was forming in my womb, I wanted to bless her. I wanted her to have the very best life possible and to know the Lord in a very intimate way.

And the desire to bless your children continues to grow every single day. But even in all my desire to give my children "good" gifts, I fail. I fall short of everything good and am left with nothing more than a desire that I am unable to fulfill. The only one that can fulfill the desire to give the best gifts to our children is Jesus.

I am so very thankful that if we ask God to bless our children and give them His best, He will do it. I love that God promises us that His Word will not return void. If we have the faith to speak God's Word, we will build the world we desire around us because His Word is living and active! God's life-giving Word is able to take entire situations and turn them around for His glory!

Is there something that you are lacking in your life? Is there something that you need that only God can provide? I am 100% certain the answer to those two questions is YES. If so, sweet sister, I encourage you to humble yourself before God right now and ask Him for His blessing to rain down upon your life. This may require some shifting on your part (attitudes, actions, etc.) to be sure that you are positioning yourself to receive the good gifts that God will give. But rest assured, He will do it!

WEEKLY CHALLENGE

Commit this week's verse to memory.

Ask God right now to give you His good gifts. You will be surprised how quickly He will manifest blessing right into the center of your world, if you will allow Him access to your heart!

Get into the habit this week of thanking God for giving you His good gifts. Continue to thank Him as if it is already done, because it is!

Write down any thoughts or prayers this week so you can keep track of how God is working in your life and the lives of others.

NOTES:

_____

_____

_____

_____

_____

_____

_____

_____

_____

_____

_____

_____

_____

_____

Week 29:
God, Our Provider
{Shall Not Want}

This week's Scripture is Psalm 34:10 (KJV):

The young lions do lack, and suffer hunger: but they that seek the Lord shall not want any good thing.

I absolutely love this verse. I remember the first time I read it as a very young believer and how God gave me a great revelation of the unlimited provision that He gives to those who take Him at His Word. This verse reminds me that, yes, we will lack things, but we don't have to lack any *good* thing so long as we call upon the Lord and seek Him.

I have found the truth in this verse to be very painstakingly true. There was a season of my life when my husband and I were expecting our first child and could barely afford to buy food for the two of us. We both worked; as a matter of fact my husband held three jobs (one full-time and two part-time), but the money was always short at the end of the month. We didn't live extravagantly, either.

I remember sitting down on the couch one day in my third trimester, very tired and hungry. Shortly after I sat down I heard my husband literally crying out to the Lord, asking Him to fill our cupboards and refrigerator with food. And as my husband was sprawled out on the floor touching the physical spaces he was asking the Lord to fill with food, I heard the phone ring.

The phone call that came through changed our lives forever. On the other end of the phone was a friend of mine who on a whim was leaving to Hawaii and said the Lord put it on her heart to give all of her food to Michael and me. I couldn't help but rejoice in the fact that although we may experience lack and hunger (physically and spiritually), it isn't because God isn't real or doesn't bless His people. Rather it reminded me that when we experience hunger and lack we need to seek God—He will always show Himself strong and provide our needs!

And over the last 15+ years He has continued to prove Psalm 34:10 true. He is faithful! Hallelujah!

WEEKLY CHALLENGE

Commit this week's verse to memory.

I encourage you to jot down some areas where you are lacking God's blessing. Begin to diligently seek Him regarding those areas and watch as He comes in and blesses you! Remember not to try and figure out how He'll bless you—just be open to receive as it never looks the way you think it will!

Pray for someone today that God will fill every area of lack in their lives with His goodness. Amen!

Write down any thoughts or prayers this week so you can keep track of how God is working in your life and the lives of others.

NOTES:

_____

_____

_____

_____

_____

_____

_____

_____

_____

_____

_____

_____

_____

_____

_____

Week 30:
God, Our Provider
{Never Forsaken}

This week's Scripture is Psalm 37:25 (KJV):

I have been young, and now am old; yet I have not seen the righteous forsaken, nor his seed begging bread.

In December of this year I am turning forty. To some this is old and to some this is young. To me, this is a very exciting time in my life where I feel like I have gained enough wisdom and insight in marriage, motherhood, and life to help others when God calls me to do so. And one thing I can say is that I have lived long enough to see the truth of Psalm 37:25 at work in countless people's lives.

I have seen many of my Christian brothers and sisters in unimaginable circumstances—and time and time again I have watched the hand of the Lord move mightily in their situations. The one key component that I have witnessed is that the person in need must have their eyes fixed upon Jesus so they do not miss the blessings He bestows upon them. As a matter of fact, I have watched the Lord move in many impossible situations in my own family and life. And every single time God provided. I've realized that He always shows up when I was seeking His glorious face rather than wallowing around in the gloom and doom of my circumstance.

Maybe you are facing an impossible situation where you feel like your family is in jeopardy of losing it all. *We've been there.* But I can tell you this: If you hold fast to the profession of your faith, God will do what His Word promises! He will not forsake you and you will not go without the necessities in life so long as you are turned toward Him.

Be sure to thank God often for the fact that we are never forsaken. Although life may not play out the way you imagine, trust and see that the Lord is good, and His beauty and provision can be found in every situation.

Weekly Challenge

Commit this week's verse to memory.

Make it a point to seek God every time you are tempted to focus on an impossible circumstance. Watch the Lord come in and move on your behalf every.single.time.

Pray for God's children to recognize His voice and heed His call so they can walk in His abundant blessing and provision.

Write down any thoughts or prayers this week so you can keep track of how God is working in your life and the lives of others.

Notes:

_____

_____

_____

_____

_____

_____

_____

_____

_____

_____

_____

_____

_____

_____

Week 31:
God, Our Provider
{Satisfy}

This week's Scripture is Psalm 145:16 (KJV):

*Thou openest thine hand, and satisfiest
the desire of every living thing.*

Psalm 145 is such an uplifting and encouraging passage to read. This passage is filled with praises and thanks to God for all He is and speaks to His faithfulness and holiness. I love verse sixteen as it talks about how God opens His hand and satisfies the desires of His creation. *And He does.*

As I read today's memory verse I am reflecting on all of the undeniable ways that the Lord has opened His hand in my life and in the lives of those around me—satisfying our deepest desires. I realized long ago that the only thing that stops God from blessing me with all that He has for me is myself. I declare today and every day that I will heed His call and position myself to receive all that God has promised me, as only He can fulfill the deepest desires of my heart!

Will you do the same today, dear sister? Will you allow the Lord to satisfy the deep longing He has put inside of your heart to serve Him and fulfill your God-given destiny? It is only through Christ that you will be able to move beyond fear and press into your purpose - all the while being satisfied in every way possible. He will provide the way, will you follow?

I am encouraged by this verse to continue to walk out my days seeking God's face and allowing Him to continuously mold me into the daughter He designed me to be. I am so grateful that the King of Kings is my daddy and that He loves me (and you!) more than we can possibly even imagine. Let's rest today in knowing that our Heavenly Father is ready to bless us and lead us right into the midst of His plan for our lives! Hallelujah!

WEEKLY CHALLENGE

Commit this week's verse to memory.

Can you think of a time or two that the Lord has opened His hand and satisfied a deep desire that you'd been trying to fill elsewhere? Share your testimony with someone else to encourage them not to give up!

Write this verse down wherever you can. Make it in plain sight so you can remember that He will open His hand for you and satisfy your deep God-given desires! He will do it! Build your faith and watch Him move in your life!

Write down any thoughts or prayers this week so you can keep track of how God is working in your life and the lives of others.

NOTES:

_____

_____

_____

_____

_____

_____

_____

_____

_____

_____

_____

_____

_____

_____

_____

Week 32:
God is my Healer
{Healed}

This week's Scripture is Isaiah 53:4-5 (KJV):

> *4 Surely he hath borne our griefs, and carried our sorrows: yet we did esteem him stricken, smitten of God, and afflicted. 5 But he was wounded for our transgressions, he was bruised for our iniquities: the chastisement of our peace was upon him; and with his stripes we are healed.*

These Scriptures have been a cornerstone of my personal faith since the day of my Salvation. You see, the day I gave my life to Christ He had to show me that He was my healer as my spirit and body were broken. For several years prior to my salvation I had been battling some serious health issues in my body that made me feel hopeless and alone. *Very alone*. But God showed me in His Word that He sent

His Son Jesus to make me whole in all things—even my body.

Is there something you are facing right now and you need hope to propel you into God's healing power? If so, I encourage you to meditate on Isaiah 53:4-5 to begin to build your faith. By meditating on this Scripture you will begin to open your heart and mind to access God's healing power in every area of your life. And as one who has experienced (and continues to experience) God's healing power, I can assure you that you won't regret positioning yourself to receive God's healing!

I want to encourage those of you who are feeling discouraged because you feel like God isn't hearing your prayers for healing—don't give up. I don't know why every person we pray for isn't healed in a physical way that we can see, but I do know that God's healing is real. And what *we consider* to be healing may not be the absolute healing and finality in a situation. Remember that God knows all and sees all and we simply do not. Our job is simply to trust and obey—God doesn't disappoint!

WEEKLY CHALLENGE

Commit this week's verse to memory.

Pray for someone this week who is in need of healing in their body. Continue to water your seed of faith by thanking God every day that it is done.

Make an attempt to visit a sick person in your family, church, or local nursing home. Encourage them by loving on them and speaking/praying God's Word over them. Even if the person isn't a Believer, you can still pray silently and speak God's life-giving words over them!

Write down any thoughts or prayers this week so you can keep track of how God is working in your life and the lives of others.

NOTES:

_____

_____

_____

_____

_____

_____

_____

_____

_____

_____

_____

_____

_____

_____

Week 33:
God is my Healer
{Life}

This week's Scripture is Proverbs 4:20-22 (KJV):

My son, attend to my words;
incline thine ear unto my sayings.
Let them not depart from thine eyes;
keep them in the midst of thine heart. For
they are life unto those that find them,
and health to all their flesh.

I will never forget the first time I was sitting in church as a newly saved young woman and my pastor began to talk about the difference between our spirit and our flesh. I was astounded. You mean I am more than just my flesh? I have a spirit *and* a soul? To be introduced to this concept was mind-boggling to say the least. That sermon was a game changer for me.

I finally made a connection that gave me insight into some of the struggles I was having in my personal life—my flesh was fighting against my spirit! And unfortunately, most of the time my flesh was winning, as I had no idea that there was even a difference between the two—until that day!

What I love so much about Proverbs 4:20-22 is that these verses give us a nugget of treasure that literally takes us to a place where we can begin to take control over our flesh. How? By allowing God's life-giving Word to heal us in the flesh and build up our faith in the spirit!

The truth contained in these verses is life-changing if you will just take hold of what God is saying and allow Him to make you whole: body, spirit, and mind. And believe me, there is no better state of mind nor place to be than right smack dab in the middle of what God has for you...and that includes making you whole!

Will you let Him bring life and health to all your flesh today, sweet sister?

WEEKLY CHALLENGE

Commit these verses to memory.

Confess (speak out loud) and think about these verses over and over until you begin to hear the Lord speak to your heart. Make it a priority to hear His voice today!

Write these verses down and post them around the house, keep them in your purse, and place them anywhere else you will see them. Make sure you get these verses into your spirit today!

Write down any thoughts or prayers this week so you can keep track of how God is working in your life and the lives of others.

NOTES:

_____

_____

_____

_____

_____

_____

_____

_____

_____

_____

_____

_____

_____

_____

WEEK 34:
GOD IS MY HEALER
{BINDETH}

This week's Scripture is Psalm 147:3 (KJV):

He healeth the broken in heart, and
bindeth up their wounds.

Have you ever experienced a broken heart? Have you ever been through a situation so painful that you literally thought you couldn't make it to the other side? I know I have. As a matter of fact, I've been through several. One situation in particular comes to mind as I type this devotional tonight.

When I was just eight years old my very best friend in the world was killed in a car accident. This friend of mine, Laura, had been a constant source of joy and escape for me during a tumultuous childhood. She could always make me laugh and smile no matter what horrible circumstances I was faced with at home.

The day Laura died I was beyond devastated. I didn't have a "safe place" anymore. I didn't have anyone that I could trust or that would love me the way I was and not judge me. I was heartbroken and I didn't know if I'd ever come out of it.

But I did.

God worked through countless people over the years to bind up my wounds and make me whole. He gave me the ability to accept Salvation through Jesus despite all the tragedies I had suffered in my short time on earth. He gave me clarity when all I saw was blurry at best. He gave me rest and peace. And eventually He restored my joy and made my life complete.

Will you let Him be your healer today?

No matter what painful circumstances you have faced or are facing today, let God bind up your wounds and make you whole. It will be one of the best decisions you will ever make!

WEEKLY CHALLENGE

Commit these verses to memory.

Allow God to bind up your deepest wounds. Give Him the ability to rearrange your heart and make it new. He is faithful to perform His Word.

Commit to praying for those you know who suffer from broken hearts. Lift them up to God and intercede on their behalf. Sometimes people are so hurt that they cannot find their way. Be a light and source of encouragement to them while they cannot stand on their own.

Write down any thoughts or prayers this week so you can keep track of how God is working in your life and the lives of others.

NOTES:

_____

_____

_____

_____

_____

_____

_____

_____

_____

_____

_____

_____

_____

Week 35:
God is my Healer
{Thy Faith}

This week's Scripture is Mark 5:34 (KJV):

*And he said unto her, Daughter, thy faith
hath made thee whole; go in peace, and
be whole of thy plague.*

Her faith has made her whole. These words resonated deeply within my soul on that dark, cool autumn evening on the campus of Washington State University. As I read these words nearly twenty years ago, I began to choke up and tears started streaming down my face. *Was it really that easy? Could my faith make me whole? At this point I had nothing to lose. Nothing.* So I decided that night I was going to put my entire trust into Jesus and see if He could make this young broken woman whole.

The results were undeniable. As I built my faith in Christ through reading His Word and praying—I was beginning to see healing take place. *Real healing.*

The type of healing that Mark 5:34 bears witness of. And through my faith I began to see twenty-two years of anger, abuse, self-loathing, denial, betrayal, drug use, and many other ungodly things begin to melt away. And then I knew. I knew for myself that this very verse would change the landscape of my entire life. *And it has.*

What do you need to be healed of, dear sister?

What is robbing you of your peace?

I challenge you to build your faith in Jesus and watch Him make you whole. I'm praying for you!

WEEKLY CHALLENGE

Commit these verses to memory.

Write down some areas of your life where you could use some peace and/or healing. Press in this week and test your faith and watch God's Word come to life in your situation!

Has God healed you of something amazing? If so, write it down and share your testimony! It not only honors God when we share what He has done (and is doing) in our lives, but it also increases our faith!

Write down any thoughts or prayers this week so you can keep track of how God is working in your life and the lives of others.

NOTES:

_____

_____

_____

_____

_____

_____

_____

_____

_____

_____

_____

_____

_____

_____

WEEK 36: CONFRONTING FEAR {SHADOW}

This week's Scripture is Psalm 23:4 (KJV):

Yea, though I walk through the valley of the shadow of death, I will fear no evil: for thou art with me; thy rod and thy staff they comfort me.

Psalm 23 is easily one of the most popular and widely quoted verses of the Bible, particularly when addressing fear. What I love so much about verse 4 is that it tells of a person (King David) that understands that while circumstances around him may be convincing his flesh to fear, God has the final say in His life. *And isn't this the truth?* Circumstances are constantly lying to us, trying to convince us to be afraid—but God's Word remains true—and so I choose to believe God's Word rather than what my current circumstances may look like.

One way that I heard this verse taught that changed my perspective was during a night of preaching by the late Kenneth E. Hagin. He was talking a lot about fear and how the enemy used it against us through lying to us, and how easily we actually believed those lies. He also made this statement about the first part of Psalm 23:4: "The shadow of a dog never bit anyone." And then it hit me like a ton of bricks! No! A shadow can't do anything as it simply has no substance or authority. It is just an imitation of something else.

Wow! So it was right then and there that I decided I didn't need to fear anything that may be presenting itself in my life: it was only a SHADOW, and in turn, it was also a lie. Simply put: *If God didn't say it, I don't believe it.* Period. And I've lived by this the past 18+ years, and it has changed my life drastically (for the better).

I encourage you to let God show you that fear has no place in your life. Let Him into your heart and mind today so you can experience the freedom that Christ has given us through Salvation!

Weekly Challenge

Commit these verses to memory.

What circumstances are you tempted to be afraid of? I challenge you to see the circumstance you are facing as a shadow and allow God to neutralize your fear by letting Him show you what the truth of His Word says about it!

Do you have an encouraging testimony of how God has delivered you from fear? Write it down and share it with at least one other person this week. Watch how God will make Himself known as you share what He has done for you.

Write down any thoughts or prayers this week so you can keep track of how God is working in your life and the lives of others.

Notes:

_____

_____

_____

_____

_____

_____

_____

_____

_____

_____

_____

_____

_____

WEEK 37:
CONFRONTING FEAR
{POWER, LOVE, SOUND MIND}

This week's Scripture is 2 Timothy 1:7 (KJV):

*For God hath not given us the spirit of
fear; but of power, and of love,
and of a sound mind.*

Have you ever been afraid? I mean really, really afraid? I know I have. I'm not talking about a healthy fear—like understanding not to touch fire because it will burn you. I'm talking about the fear that scares you into thinking you can't do anything right—the fear that cripples you when you try to take things to the next level in your life. I'm speaking of the fear that tells you that you are a failure, so you spend your life never trying.

There have been several circumstances in my life that made me fearful. Those who have experienced fear truly understand that fear can drive a person crazy. Fear also robs us of what God has for us because it distracts us from focusing on what God says and leaves us empty, stuck and never moving forward in our lives.

Perhaps you have been stuck in fear for a while—or you are tempted to fear right now. I have some amazing news for you: GOD HAS NOT GIVEN US A SPIRIT OF FEAR! So that means that we don't have to accept fear and all the lies that it brings.

How many times has fear talked you out of your blessing? How many times has fear told you that you will never succeed? I know fear has held me back for far too long and I refuse to allow the spirit of fear to do anything in my life. *No more!*

The beautiful thing about what God has done for us is He has given us a spirit of power, love, and a sound mind! I am giving God full permission to have His way in my life and drive out the spirit of fear at first sight. *Will you do the same?*

Weekly Challenge

Commit these verses to memory.

Write down any areas of your life in which fear has held you back. Surrender those areas to God today and ask Him to fill them with His spirit of power, His love, and a sound mind! Watch how He takes care of you and gives you exactly what you need!

Think of a time that God has given you power, love, and/or a sound mind in place of fear. Thank Him and praise Him for all He has done in your life to deliver you and protect you from fear.

Write down any thoughts or prayers this week so you can keep track of how God is working in your life and the lives of others.

NOTES:

_____

_____

_____

_____

_____

_____

_____

_____

_____

_____

_____

_____

_____

_____

Week 38:
Confronting Fear
{Love}

This week's Scripture is 1 John 4:18 (KJV):

There is no fear in love; but perfect love casteth out fear: because fear hath torment. He that feareth is not made perfect in love.

Can I get an Amen? I mean *really*. The truth of this verse resonates deep within my soul. Fear does torment us! *It really does*. I cannot tell you how crippled I was by fear as a child. I was literally tormented by demonic spirits that made me have morbid thoughts, nightmares, and even made me feel their evil presence. And as a young girl I didn't live in a home where anyone knew the Lord nor His saving power! I was going through this alone—terrified by what I'd see at night in my bed. Mortified by what presence I would feel while alone in my room. Tormented by horrible dreams that were straight out of a horror film. It was a very hard period of my life. But then I met LOVE.

When I met Jesus He showed me that LOVE and fear do not co-exist, because fear torments. Now don't get me wrong, there is a difference between tormenting fear and a fear that is reverence for a Holy God. A reverent fear is one of respect and honor—nothing dangerous or fear-based. Now I am not talking about a blind following of someone or something—rather I am talking about revering God for who He is in your life. And in that understanding there is FREEDOM from the torment and lies the enemy slings your way! Hallelujah!

Let's commit together to kicking out fear for good and embracing God's love to the fullest! With Him, we can do this!

WEEKLY CHALLENGE

Commit this week's verse to memory.

Do you have any areas of your life where fear keeps you bound? If so, talk to a pastor or loved one about this and ask them to pray with you in agreement that fear will leave once and for all!

Speak this Scripture out loud daily. Watch as your faith builds and God's love rises up within you, driving out fear and giving you God's peace instead!

Write down any thoughts or prayers this week so you can keep track of how God is working in your life and the lives of others.

NOTES:

_____

_____

_____

_____

_____

_____

_____

_____

_____

_____

_____

_____

_____

_____

_____

_____

WEEK 39: CONFRONTING FEAR {FEAR NOT}

This week's Scripture is Isaiah 41:10 (KJV):

Fear thou not; for I am with thee: be
not dismayed ; for I am thy God: I will
strengthen thee; yea, I will help thee; yea,
I will uphold thee with the right hand of
my righteousness.

I find so much comfort in the words above. There is something very settling in my spirit every time I read this passage of Scripture. I can tell you one thing for sure: God has strengthened me through many times where fear nearly claimed my life.

Has fear ever driven you to a place that you felt as if your very life was being stolen from you?

Be encouraged, dear sister, God promises to be with us, help us, and literally uphold us with the right hand of His righteousness. What a mighty God we serve!

The next time you are tempted to succumb to fear, remember the promises contained within Isaiah 41:10. If you keep this at the threshold of your faith, you will certainly overcome any fear that the enemy throws your way! You will not only overcome fear through your faith—giving God access to fight your battles—you will also walk in His victory! And there is nothing sweeter than being on God's winning team!

WEEKLY CHALLENGE

Commit this week's verse to memory.

Confront an area of your life where you have been afraid. Walk through this verse in every aspect of the circumstance and watch God dissipate the fear right out of you and your situation!

Pray for a friend or family member who is seemingly crippled by fear. Speak God's Word of life over them. Write out the memory verses from this month and give it to them to speak to their fear.

Write down any thoughts or prayers this week so you can keep track of how God is working in your life and the lives of others.

NOTES:

_____

_____

_____

_____

_____

_____

_____

_____

_____

_____

_____

_____

_____

_____

WEEK 40: RESTING IN HIM {COME}

This week's Scripture is Matthew 11:28 (KJV):

Come unto me, all ye that labour and are heavy laden, and I will give you rest.

This has to be one of the most calming Scriptures I have ever read in my life. There is something to take note of when an Almighty God tells you that He will give you rest. In *Strong's Concordance*, *rest* in the Greek is *anapauó*, which means to give rest or to give intermission from labor.

Did you see that? He promises to give us rest, the type of rest that anyone who has lived into adulthood understands to be life-giving rest, if we simply *come.*

I remember the first time I realized what I had to do in order to gain rest from the hard labor of the life I was living. Although it sounds easy enough to just "come" to God and enter into His rest, it isn't quite as simple as you'd think. I have found in my journey with Christ that it's in the "coming" that we find a battle of it's own awaiting us to fight.

What do I mean? I mean the attacks that come immediately when you set your mind on following His will. I am talking about looking yourself in the mirror and being honest with who you are and where you are really at. And trust me, it is never easy, no matter how often you do it. But the thing is, in order to enter into His rest, you have to.

And every battle I fight in order to rest in God's promise of refreshing is worth its weight in gold. If you are in the midst of a battle for rest, I encourage you to stay grounded in Him and don't give up. God promises you that He will give you rest, and He will do it. Just hold on to His Word and He will sustain you. And before you know it, your rest will come!

Weekly Challenge

Commit this week's verse to memory.

Figure out what you need to do in order to submit yourself to God and enter into His rest. Pray and ask God for the strength to carry on and thank Him in advance for the promise of rest that is on its way!

Pray and ask God if you can be of service to help someone else enter into His rest. You'll be surprised at the outcome, I guarantee it!

Write down any thoughts or prayers this week so you can keep track of how God is working in your life and the lives of others.

NOTES:

_____

_____

_____

_____

_____

_____

_____

_____

_____

_____

_____

_____

_____

_____

WEEK 41:
RESTING IN HIM
{WITH THEE}

This week's Scripture is Exodus 33:14 (KJV):

And he said, My presence shall go [with thee], and I will give thee rest.

In the earlier part of Exodus 33, Moses was talking to the Lord and the Lord told him that he had found favor in His sight. Moses then began asking the Lord to show him His ways so that He may know the Lord more and continue to find favor in His sight. And then the Lord replied with the verse above (Exodus 33:14), telling Moses that His presence would go with him and He would give Moses rest.

The *Strong's Exhaustive Concordance* tells us that *rest* in this verse in the Greek is:

> *nûwach, noo'-akh*; a primitive root; to rest, i.e. settle down; used in a great variety of applications, literal and figurative, intransitive, transitive and causative (to dwell, stay, let fall, place, let

alone, withdraw, give comfort, etc.):—
cease, be confederate, lay, let down,
(be) quiet, remain, (cause to, be at, give,
have, make to) rest, set down.

Wow! Reading this definition blesses me to the core! This gives us a pretty clear indication of the wonderful rest that God will grant to His children, if we simply trust and obey. There is something very comforting about knowing your God promises you absolute rest if you will just trust Him and His ways. But this isn't always easy.

Are you feeling like you need to hear the Lord's voice and would give anything to rest in His presence? If so, I encourage you to ask the Lord for His favor today and listen closely to His reply by staying immersed in both the reading of His Word and prayer. I promise you this: God will not let you down; as a matter of fact, He will give you what you seek!

Weekly Challenge

Commit this week's verse to memory.

Ask the Lord today for His favor and the ability to enter into His rest. Pray for others who are weary that they also be granted the favor of the Lord and the ability to rest.

Make it a point to write this verse down on paper, post-it notes, mirrors, or any other place that you will see it. This is a great tool for memorization!

Write down any thoughts or prayers this week so you can keep track of how God is working in your life and the lives of others.

NOTES:

_____

_____

_____

_____

_____

_____

_____

_____

_____

_____

_____

_____

_____

_____

Week 42:
Resting in Him
{Remaineth}

This week's Scripture is Hebrews 4:9 (KJV):

There remaineth therefore a rest to the people of God.

Do you believe this? Do you believe that there is a rest for God's people? Because there is. I've entered into it myself, and there is no greater feeling than to be at rest in His presence.

What is it that you are weary from, sweet sister? Is it the things of this world? Your job? The lies of the media? Financial struggles? Marital issues? Motherhood? The enemy of your soul? I'll bet there are a lot of things that are preventing you from entering into the rest that God has called you to. But hear this: Even though you are busy, you are never too busy to enter into the planned rest that God has predestined for each one of us.

Remember that physical rest is only one aspect of this verse. *But spiritual rest—peace of mind—is a major component of whether or not the other part of rest (physical) can be fulfilled.*

What is it that you need to do today to get more time with the King of Kings? How can you be committed to entering into His rest?

Ask Him to show you where you need rest and allow Him to give you the wisdom to get there. Let's make it a point to enter into His rest this week. And watch everything around you become less tiring, your relationships more loving, and your relationship with God become more powerful!

Be sure to remain in His rest, too. Don't just go back to your old ways. Really trust that He wants you to be at rest in His presence. I'll meet you there!

WEEKLY CHALLENGE

Commit this week's verse to memory.

Write down the things in your life that you perceive to make you the most tired. After you write your list—pray and ask God to show you where you can change up your routines to find more time with Him.

Make it a point to make some choices this week that will make you less physically tired. If you go to bed late, try heading to bed a bit earlier. If you eat a lot of sweets, try cutting back and drinking more water. There are plenty of things we can all do to help make our physical bodies more rested.

Write down any thoughts or prayers this week so you can keep track of how God is working in your life and the lives of others.

Notes:

Week 43: Resting in Him {Labour}

This week's Scripture is Hebrews 4:11 (KJV):

Let us labour therefore to enter into that rest, lest any man fall after the same example of unbelief.

Hebrews 4 is all about the importance of entering into the rest that God has provided for His people. This rest is a much-needed rest to restore the body, mind, and spirit. I am sure you understand that when we run around constantly working and serving, we are not able to be filled with His peace and presence. Don't get me wrong: I am in no way suggesting that you should sit around and do nothing. Rather I am saying that the Lord wants us to rest in order to remain strong in body, soul, and spirit.

I encourage you today to be obedient to the call for rest that God declares upon His people. Don't ignore the importance of rest for those who labor to the glory of God. We need to be sure that we make time to rest in His presence and allow for the nourishment that only He can provide for our spirit, body, and soul.

It is in this rest that you will find more fuel for the journey. Resting in His presence will enable you to be filled up after giving so much. Entering into God's rest will also allow you to experience more of Him - giving you a new level of understanding to share with those He's called you to minister to.

If you haven't already, dear sister, enter into His rest and watch the Spirit of God do an even mightier work in and through you!

Weekly Challenge

Commit this week's verse to memory.

Make it an absolute point this week to find an area that you need to be more "restful" in. Everyone's life looks different, so don't try and compare your "rest" to anyone else. Rather, determine the area that you need it and be obedient—and rest.

Pray and ask God how you can help assist someone in their need to rest. You will be surprised at the unique ways the Lord will use you to bless one of His people who is in need of entering into His rest.

Write down any thoughts or prayers this week so you can keep track of how God is working in your life and the lives of others.

NOTES:

_____

_____

_____

_____

_____

_____

_____

_____

_____

_____

_____

_____

_____

_____

Week 44:
Resting in Him
{Beloved}

This week's Scripture is Psalm 127:2 (KJV):

It is vain for you to rise up early, to sit up late, to eat the bread of sorrows: for so he giveth his beloved sleep.

In studying Psalm 127:2 back in my college days, I realized one amazing truth about this verse: It has very little to do with physical sleep and more to do with trusting the Lord. I learned that in order to enter into His rest, trust is key. What this verse is teaching us is that rather than being worrisome and toiling for all we have, why do we not enter into His rest? It's a simple question with a very complex answer that will vary from person to person. However, it is something we must all ask ourselves. And there is a way to obtain the beloved sleep that God promises in this verse.

To be clear, I am not suggesting that one should not work for a living, nor am I saying that we should be lazy and wait for God's blessing to fall into our lap. Rather I am saying that in order to rest in Christ, we must first learn to trust that He is who He says He is.

Once we submit ourselves to Him, we are able to rest in knowing that He will provide our every need if we just listen to His voice. So instead of toiling, let us be guided by His voice so our work is not in vain and our rest is the kind of sweet, beloved sleep that only He can give.

Who's with me?

Will you make it a point to submit every area of your life to Christ today in order to experience that beloved sleep that He gives to His children? This isn't an easy feat and we will continuously have to search our hearts in order to remain in His rest, but as long as we are committed to Him, He will never let us down!

Weekly Challenge

Commit this week's verse to memory.

Identify some areas of your life where trust is lacking in your relationship with God. Submit those areas to God and pray and ask Him to show you exactly how you can enter into the beloved sleep His Word promises His children.

Pray and ask the Lord to show you someone who is in need of entering into His rest. Be a light to them and share with them God's message of hope and Scriptures that we've been memorizing this month!

Write down any thoughts or prayers this week so you can keep track of how God is working in your life and the lives of others.

NOTES:

_____

_____

_____

_____

_____

_____

_____

_____

_____

_____

_____

_____

_____

_____

Week 45:
God's Peace
{Perfect}

This week's Scripture is Isaiah 26:3 (KJV):

Thou wilt keep him in perfect peace,
whose mind is stayed on thee: because
he trusteth in thee.

Trust isn't something that comes easily to me. To be honest, my personality is pretty much programmed to trust very few people. I had to learn in my walk with God to let go of the fleshly impulses to base my trust off of what I could see and allow myself to fall freely into the arms of my Savior. And from the very first moment I let all of my inhibition go—I felt the peace of God.

In my experience, there is nothing that can compare to God's peace. *Nothing at all.* No amount of material things, worldly accolades, or human companionship is like the peace of God. While the amazing family I've been blessed with and the love we share comes at a close second—God's peace still trumps everything.

Peace in Hebrew is *shalom. Shalom* means "nothing missing, nothing broken". In other words, God's peace is the absolute fulfillment of our human mind, body, and soul. *Doesn't this sound divine?*

And the fact that His Word promises us that if we focus on Him and trust in Him that He will keep us in perfect peace is absolutely astounding.

I encourage you (as I encourage myself) to do whatever you need to do to keep Jesus at the forefront of your thoughts, keeping Him and His Word as the crux of your life. And in doing so you will walk in His peace—which means you will be complete, lacking nothing.

Weekly Challenge

Commit this week's verse to memory.

Do you have God's peace as a regular part of your life? If so, continue to focus on Him to remain at peace. If not, make it a point this week to meditate on this Scripture and keep Jesus as the first thing you focus on when you wake up, throughout the day, and before you go to sleep. Watch as God's peace will fill your heart and mind, making the everyday stresses of life seem minuscule.

Pray for God's peace to infiltrate everywhere you go. Peace can lead you in your day-to-day life as well as minister to those around you.

Write down any thoughts or prayers this week so you can keep track of how God is working in your life and the lives of others.

Notes:

_____

_____

_____

_____

_____

_____

_____

_____

_____

_____

_____

_____

_____

Week 46:
God's Peace
{Christ Jesus}

This week's Scripture is Philippians 4:7 (KJV):

And the peace of God, which passeth all understanding, shall keep your hearts and minds through Christ Jesus.

Have you ever felt like you were losing your mind? Has your heart hurt so badly that you felt as if you couldn't go on? I've been there, too. I've also experienced the truth of Philippians 4:7, giving me hope in situations that were seemingly impossible. I've prayed and spoken this verse to my circumstances and it changed them every time.

Today if you are feeling as if you are going to lose your mind and are suffering from a broken heart, I encourage you to meditate on Philippians 4:7, reading and speaking it out loud over and over again. I know it might seem strange at first to some, but the Bible tells us in Romans 10:17:

So then faith cometh by hearing, and hearing by the word of God.

So when you read God's Word aloud, you are building your own faith by reading, speaking, and hearing God's Word all at once! That is something, isn't it?

God's peace is available to you today, sweet sister. All you have to do is keep your mind on Him and His Word and He promises you will have a peace like no other.

I am praying for you, dear sister. Be encouraged and know that God's peace is not only real, it is also for you to experience even in the most difficult times of your life.

WEEKLY CHALLENGE

Commit this week's verse to memory.

Take the time at least once a day to read this week's verse out loud several times. Pray that God will build your faith while you take a step in obedience to His word.

Share this verse with someone who could use God's peace in their lives.

Write down any thoughts or prayers this week so you can keep track of how God is working in your life and the lives of others.

NOTES:

_____

_____

_____

_____

_____

_____

_____

_____

_____

_____

_____

_____

_____

_____

Week 47:
God's Peace
{Overcome}

This week's Scripture is John 16:33 (KJV):

These things I have spoken unto you, that in me ye might have peace. In the world ye shall have tribulation: but be of good cheer; I have overcome the world.

I cannot count how many times this particular verse of Scripture has helped change my mindset when faced with a difficult day or season of life. When I read John 16:33, I can't help but be thrilled that the King of Kings is speaking directly to me (and to all of His people), letting us know that even though things may get hard, His promises remain true. This, dear sister, is something to smile about.

Maybe you are in a season where you feel like the world around you is crashing down. Perhaps you are facing the daunting consequence of a poor decision, or the pain of a debilitating disease. Whatever you are facing today, take great peace in knowing that when it is all said and done, Jesus has paid the price for your sin. But also remember that the peace you seek is only found in Him. We must seek His face through prayer, Bible reading, and praise and worship. No matter how you seek Him, just make sure that you do. He won't let you down!

The next time you are faced with a circumstance that is seemingly impossible to overcome, remember that Jesus has overcome the world. And that, dear one, is something to be happy about.

Will you let His peace into your life today?

WEEKLY CHALLENGE

Commit this week's verse to memory.

Identify at least three key areas of your life where you need to allow God's peace to come in and change your circumstances. Write these key areas down and pray about them. As God begins to work in these areas, go back and write in your testimony and use it to encourage yourself and others!

Are you a part of a Christian community that can help hold you accountable? If so, ask your fellow Christians to pray for you to be strengthened in the area of accepting God's peace. Even though His peace is available to us, we don't always allow our hearts to be open to receive it. I know you will see an increase in both faith and peace as your fellow brothers and sisters pray for you. If you aren't currently part of a local community, there are many places you can seek online prayer. I encourage you to find one and submit a prayer request.

Write down any thoughts or prayers this week so you can keep track of how God is working in your life and the lives of others.

NOTES:

_____

_____

_____

_____

_____

_____

_____

_____

_____

_____

_____

_____

_____

Week 48:
God's Peace
{Hope & Power}

This week's Scripture is Romans 15:13 (KJV):

Now the God of hope fill you with all joy and peace in believing, that ye may abound in hope, through the power of the Holy Ghost.

In the early morning hours of September 14, 1998, the Lord showed me the importance of His peace. The night before, I had some very disturbing spiritual experiences. Let's just say that it wasn't the Lord that visited me in those wee hours of the night. As a young believer, not only was I tempted to be afraid, but I was also questioning whether or not I had made the right choice earlier that week to accept Jesus as my Savior. But as I prayed and read the Bible, God showed up in a very unforgettable way. And the first thing He told me was, "Seek my peace."

It wasn't until several months later that I had a more complete picture of why God's peace is so important. Romans 15:13 sums much of it up quite well, sharing that God will not only fill us with joy and peace as we believe in Him, but that we will abound in hope through the power of the Holy Spirit. This is something. Really something.

Why? Because it is hope that helps us make it to another day. It is the power of the Holy Spirit that gives us the ability to break free from our circumstances. And this, dear one, produces a peace that is undeniable.

Will you believe God today? Will you take Him at His Word? If you choose to do so, you will begin to experience a new level of peace that you didn't even know existed. Hallelujah!

WEEKLY CHALLENGE

Commit this week's verse to memory.

This week when you are faced with a situation that takes your focus away from God, speak this verse aloud several times until your peace is restored. It has been my experience that the Word of God heals and gives us the grace we need for today and the hope we need for tomorrow.

Pray for ways to model God's peace in your family and community. Let Him show you people that need His peace, and offer to pray for them. This will not only honor God and lift up your fellow brothers and sisters, but it will also increase your own faith.

Write down any thoughts or prayers this week so you can keep track of how God is working in your life and the lives of others.

NOTES:

_____

_____

_____

_____

_____

_____

_____

_____

_____

_____

_____

_____

_____

_____

Week 49:
Live to Give
{Bless}

This week's Scripture is Deuteronomy 15:10 (KJV):

Thou shalt surely give him, and
thine heart shall not be grieved when
thou givest unto him: because that for
this thing the Lord thy God shall
bless thee in all thy works, and in all that
thou puttest thine hand unto.

Giving without expectation is something that truly brings my heart great joy. But it wasn't always this way. Growing up there were many times that I wondered if I was going to have a meal to eat. I remember becoming accustomed to only eating at school, and dreading the summer when those "for sure" meals would end. I found myself measuring everything when I was "sharing" food. Even in college I would get eye-level with a glass if I was pouring a beverage for a friend and me—to make sure that I had more. I was always afraid that there wouldn't be any "more," and it stole the joy of giving from me at a very early age.

But then I met Jesus. And everything changed. *For the good.*

Once I accepted the gift that God gave us in His son Jesus, I realized that I wasn't as stingy as I had thought. I realized that life had beaten me down and made me believe I was someone that I really wasn't. Then God began to rebuild my understanding of who He created me to be, and how He has gifted me with the anointing to give. And it gave me an unspeakable freedom and joy to know that by doing what I love to do—give—He will bless me in all I do. And I don't do it for the blessing. I do it because it feels so good to give without expectation.

I am so thankful that God got a hold of me some nearly twenty years ago to teach me this freeing truth: *Giving without expectation makes the heart full.*

And so, dear friend, I pray that you have found the same freedom in this truth. And I pray that you also find comfort in the promises contained in Deuteronomy 15:10. Rest in this, dear one, as it will give you hope on the days you feel like giving up. Peace and joy on the days that life tries to rob you of your promise. Assurance that He who promised is faithful. Amen!

WEEKLY CHALLENGE

Commit this week's verse to memory.

Do you give without expectation? If so, how does that make you feel? If not, what is something you can do to help change your heart when it comes to giving?

Make a point to give to someone special this week— someone to whom you wouldn't normally think to give. Giving can be sharing your time, making a meal, being a listening ear, or even giving financial blessing. Whatever your heart is led to give, just do it. You will not only be the hands and feet of Jesus, but you will also feel amazing.

Write down any thoughts or prayers this week so you can keep track of how God is working in your life and the lives of others.

NOTES:

_____

_____

_____

_____

_____

_____

_____

_____

_____

_____

_____

_____

_____

_____

WEEK 50: LIVE TO GIVE {LIFE}

This week's Scripture is John 3:16 (KJV):

For God so loved the world,
that he gave his only begotten Son, that
whosoever believeth in him should not
perish, but have everlasting life.

The ultimate gift giver is clearly our God. I mean, who could ever possibly give us a gift better than the irreplaceable, one-of-a-kind gift, His Son Jesus? I often sit and try to wrap my human mind around this gift and just simply cannot do so. And so instead of trying to fathom it, I do my very best to mimic it with the blessings that God has given me. And there are many gifts that He has given me—and you, dear sister. For starters, the gift of life. And with this one gift, the gift of life, we can do so many wonderful things.

I encourage you to continuously ask the Lord what gift He wants you to share with His people. I think you'll be rather surprised by His answers. Over the years as I've tried to model my giving around the ultimate gift, God has shown me so much about myself and the gifts that He has placed inside of me.

It's amazing that as we seek Him we find the hidden treasures that He has put inside of each one of us. I am so encouraged as I see each of God's people moving forward in the gifts He has placed within them. One of the most beautiful sights to behold is when I see one of God's people doing what He created them to do. There's just nothing quite like it.

What is the gift(s) that God is asking you to move forward with?

What, if anything, is preventing you from doing so?

I encourage you, sweet sister of mine, to allow the King of Kings to shine through all you do. Don't let fear hold you back and try to steal the gift you've been given in Christ—the gift of new life and freedom. I'm praying for you as you continue to do your very best to give from what you have been given. Never forget that we can do all things through Christ Jesus!

WEEKLY CHALLENGE

Commit this week's verse to memory.

Find one way you can use your gift of Salvation to bless another person this week. Pray and ask God for guidance as you continue to give out of the abundant gift He gave us in Christ Jesus.

Share with someone about the gift of Jesus. Share your testimony with another person and watch as God opens their heart to receive His gift of life!

Write down any thoughts or prayers this week so you can keep track of how God is working in your life and the lives of others.

NOTES:

_____

_____

_____

_____

_____

_____

_____

_____

_____

_____

_____

_____

_____

Week 51:
Live to Give
{Withhold Not}

This week's Scripture is Proverbs 3:27 (KJV):

*Withhold not good from them to whom it
is due, when it is in the power
of thine hand to do it.*

I remember the first time I read this verse, and it rocked me to the core. The afternoon prior to reading this Scripture for the very first time, I had done just the opposite of what it said. Another college-aged girl who lived in my apartment complex had asked me for money because she didn't have food. I have to be honest—I couldn't give her any money because I only had pennies in my less-than-full checking account. And truthfully, I knew I wasn't supposed to give her money. But I did hear a still small voice telling me to invite her over for dinner that night. But I ignored it. I was tired and had to study for three finals and work a full shift at work. Needless to say, I still could have had her over.

I am not suggesting that we break our backs and neglect our own responsibilities when someone else is in need. I don't believe that is what this Scripture is saying. Rather, I believe God is trying to communicate to us that it isn't Christ-like to sit and watch someone suffer when we are able to do something about it.

For instance, maybe there is a local family going through a hard transition right now (such as job loss, death in the family, sickness, etc.); the simple act of bringing them a meal could do wonders for their morale. Or maybe there is a woman you see day in and day out who just looks sad; perhaps you can ask her if you can pray for her, or just smile and say hello. It is these things that I believe the Lord is speaking about—the everyday acts of kindness that we each hold in our possession to give.

Will you do your best to not withhold good from those who need it today?

I know I want to always do my best to try and give what I can. After all, I was given the gift of eternal life through Jesus, and I don't want to neglect sharing a bit of Him everywhere I go. Will you join me in doing so? Let's go forth and be the light of Christ as we prayerfully receive His grace and do our best to follow His will.

Weekly Challenge

Commit this week's verse to memory.

Find someone who is in need this week and bless them. It doesn't have to be monetary—just help meet a need they have. Watch as God works through you to show them a piece of His love. I guarantee you will not regret it.

Gather a group of family or friends (or both) and ask them if they'd like to go on a mission this week to bless people in your communities. It's amazing what can be done in numbers—especially when God is in the midst!

Write down any thoughts or prayers this week so you can keep track of how God is working in your life and the lives of others.

Notes:

_____

_____

_____

_____

_____

_____

_____

_____

_____

_____

_____

_____

_____

NOTES:

_____

_____

_____

_____

_____

_____

_____

_____

_____

_____

_____

_____

_____

_____

_____

Week 52:
Live to Give
{Reward Thee Openly}

This week's Scripture is Matthew 6:3-4 (KJV):

*But when thou doest alms, let not thy left
hand know what thy right hand doeth:
That thine alms may be in secret: and thy
Father which seeth in secret himself
shall reward thee openly.*

This verse is packed full of need-to-know wisdom when it comes to having the spirit of a Christ-like giver. I think one of the biggest temptations we face when it comes to giving is the human need for recognition. While recognition may not be a huge struggle in your life, it is in fact a struggle that we all face. So let's take the wisdom of this verse and apply it in a practical way when we give.

What do I mean?

For me, this verse clearly gives the insight that when we give, we are to use discretion on whether we share that information with anyone outside of those we trust. For me, I will always share what I give with my husband because we share our bank account, but not necessarily with anyone else.

This verse also shows me that giving is more about doing what is right in the eyes of the Lord than anything else. God isn't pleased if we go around telling everyone how much we give (whether it be money, time, or something else). Rather, Matthew 6:3-4 teaches that it is pleasing to Him when we give in secret. And He is so pleased about this that He will reward us openly. Just know that the reward likely won't come in the form you expect—it is more that His blessing will be evident in our lives. And this, dear sister, is what it is all about: *Showing the world Jesus through our lives.*

Let's make it a point to keep our hearts in check when it comes to our giving. Be honest with where you are at in this, and God will strengthen you to become more like Him in this area. Amen!

WEEKLY CHALLENGE

Commit this week's verse to memory.

Do you struggle with letting others know about your giving? If so, I encourage you to ask the Lord to help you see what you can change in order to be made whole in this area.

How has the Lord rewarded you openly for your giving? Write down your testimony and share it with someone who may struggle with giving to others. It may be just the nudge they need to break free from their bondage and walk into the freedom of Christ-like giving!

Write down any thoughts or prayers this week so you can keep track of how God is working in your life and the lives of others.

Notes:

_____

_____

_____

_____

_____

_____

_____

_____

_____

_____

_____

_____

_____

_____

_____

About the Author

Carlie Kercheval is a happily married wife, mom of three fantastic children, lover of the outdoors, and creative at heart. You can learn more about Carlie and her various projects on any of her websites:

Learning to Speak Life Books™
store.learningtospeaklife.com

Fulfilling Your Vows™
fulfillingyourvows.com

Today's Frugal Mom™
todaysfrugalmom.com

Are you on social media?
You can connect with her on:

Instagram
instagram.com/carliekercheval

Pinterest
pinterest.com/carliekercheval

Made in the USA
San Bernardino, CA
12 August 2016